Pope Francis

MORNING HOMILIES III

POPE FRANCIS

MORNING HOMILIES III

In the Chapel of St. Martha's Guest House
February 3 – June 30, 2014

Translated by Dinah Livingstone

ORBIS BOOKS
Maryknoll, New York 10545

Founded in 1970, Orbis Books endeavors to publish works that enlighten the mind, nourish the spirit, and challenge the conscience. The publishing arm of the Maryknoll Fathers and Brothers, Orbis seeks to explore the global dimensions of the Christian faith and mission, to invite dialogue with diverse cultures and religious traditions, and to serve the cause of reconciliation and peace. The books published reflect the views of their authors and do not represent the official position of the Maryknoll Society. To learn more about Maryknoll and Orbis Books, please visit our website at www.maryknollsociety.org.

Translation copyright © 2016 by Orbis Books
Published by Orbis Books, Box 302, Maryknoll, NY 10545-0302.
All rights reserved.

Originally published as *Le parole di Papa Francesco* OMELIE DEL MATTINO *nella Cappella della Domus Sanctae Marthaem, 3 febbraio - 30 giugno 2014* © 2014 by Libreria Editrice Vaticana. (From original summaries published in *L'Osservatore Romano*, used with permission.)

Queries regarding rights and permissions should be addressed to: Orbis Books, P.O. Box 302, Maryknoll, NY 10545-0302.

Manufactured in the United States of America
Design: Roberta Savage

Library of Congress Cataloging in Publication

Francis, Pope, 1936-
[Sermons. Selections. English]
Pope Francis morning homilies : in the Chapel of St. Martha's guest house / translated by Dinah Livingstone.
3 volumes cm
Contents: I. 22 March-6 July 2013 II. 2 September 2013-31 January 2014 III. 3 February-30 June 2014
ISBN 978-1-62698-111-9 (v. 1: pbk.)
ISBN 978-1-62698-147-8 (v. 2 : pbk.)
ISBN 978-1-62698-179-9 (v. 3 : pbk.)
1. Catholic Church—Sermons. I. Title.
  BX1756.F677S4713 2015
  252'.02—dc23
  2014033307

Contents

Preface

Each morning Pope Francis begins his day by celebrating Mass in the chapel of Casa Santa Marta, the Vatican guest house where he has chosen to live. Those in attendance vary, including other residents and staff, curial officials, visiting dignitaries, foreign bishops, representatives of religious congregations, or others who contribute to the daily upkeep of the Vatican, such as postal workers, gardeners, and the waste collection staff. This volume of the Pope's *Morning Homilies*, the third in an ongoing series, is again based on the accounts published each day in *L'Osservatore Romano*. Through these accounts it is possible for those not present to experience and enjoy the Pope's lively manner of speaking and his capacity to engage his listeners and their daily lives.

We know what great significance Pope Francis attaches to preaching. In his apostolic exhortation *Evangelii Gaudium* he dedicated an entire chapter to the homily, *the touchstone for judging a pastor's closeness and ability to communicate to his people* (*EG* 125). There he provided numerous guidelines for effective preaching, noting that the homily *should be brief and avoid taking on the semblance of a speech or a lecture; it should be positive, not so much concerned with pointing out what shouldn't be done, but with suggesting what we can do better*; it should respect the original intent of the text (*If a text was written to console, it should not be used to correct errors*); it should avoid *abstract truths and cold syllogisms* and it should make effective use of imagery. (Here he reinforced his point by recalling the words of an old teacher, who taught

INSTRUCTIONS FOR WHEN IT'S DARK

Monday, February 3, 2014
Sᴀᴍ II 5:13-14, 30; 16:5-13ᴀ

At life's difficult moments we shouldn't "do a deal with God," or use others to save ourselves. The right attitude is to do penance, recognizing our own sins and entrusting ourselves to the Lord, without giving in to the temptation to "take the law into our own hands." At the Mass celebrated on Monday morning, February 3, in the chapel of St. Martha's Guest House, Pope Francis reconsidered the witness of King David, "saint and sinner," in the "dark moment" of his flight from Jerusalem because he had been betrayed by his son Absalom. At the end of the celebration, on this feast day of St. Blaise, two priests gave the pope and all those present the traditional blessing with two candles placed on the throat in the form of a cross.

For his meditation the pope took his cue from the first reading, taken from the second book of Samuel (15:13-14, 30; 16:5-13a). "We heard the story," he said, "of that very sad moment for David when he had to flee because his son had betrayed him." David's words are eloquent when he speaks of Absalom as "the son who came from my loins." Here we are seeing "a great betrayal." The majority of the people also go with "the son against the king." In fact we read in the biblical story: "The hearts of

3

the Israelites have gone after Absalom." Indeed, for David it was "as if this son were dead."

But what does David do when faced with Absalom's betrayal? The pope pointed out three things. First, "David, a ruler, takes the situation for what it is. He knows that this will be a savage war, that many of the people will die," because it's "one side of the people against the other." And he acts with realism, "choosing not to let his people die." Of course he could have "fought in Jerusalem against his son's forces. But he said: No, I don't want Jerusalem to be destroyed!" And he went against his men who wanted to take away the ark, ordering them to leave it where it was: "Let the ark of God remain in the city!" All this demonstrates David's "first attitude," which "doesn't use God or his people to defend himself," because of "his great love for them."

"At life's bad moments," noted the pope, "it may happen that in our desperation we try to defend ourselves in any way we can," even "using God and other people." But David shows us "his first attitude," which is "not to use God or his people."

David's second response is "a penitential attitude," which he adopts when he's fleeing from Jerusalem. In the passage from the book of Samuel, David "went weeping" up the mountain and "he went with his head covered and walking barefoot." But, commented the pope, "think what it means to go up the mountain barefoot!" And the people who were with him also went barefoot: "They covered their heads and went up, weeping as they went."

This was "a penitential road." Perhaps, continued the pope, at that moment David was thinking about the "many wrong things" and "all the sins he had committed." And he probably said to himself: "But I'm not innocent! It's not right that my son should do this to me, but I'm no saint myself!" In this spirit David "chooses penance, he weeps and does penance." His "climb up the mountain," the pope also noted, "makes us think of Jesus' own climb up a mountain. He too went painfully, barefoot, carrying his cross, up the mountain."

So David displays "a penitential attitude." But, said the pope, "when something of the sort happens in our own lives, we always try—instinctively—to justify ourselves." On the other hand, "David doesn't justify himself. He's realistic. He tries to save the ark of God and his people. He does penance," by climbing the mountain. That's why "he's a great man: a great sinner and a great saint." Of course, added the Holy Father, "God only knows how these two things go together. But it's the truth!"

Along his penitential way the king met a man called Shimei, who "threw stones" at him and his companions. He was "an enemy" who cursed David and "swore at him." So Abishai, "one of David's friends," suggests to the king that he should get him and kill him, "this dead dog," Abishai called him in the language of his time, meaning that Shimei was "a bad person." But David stops him and "instead of choosing to avenge himself for all those insults, he chooses to entrust himself to God." In the biblical passage we read: "My own son who came from my loins seeks my life, how much more now may this Benjaminite!—this Shimei! Let him alone and let him curse, for the Lord has bidden him. It may be that the Lord will look on my distress and the Lord will repay me with good for this cursing of me today." So that's David's third attitude: he "entrusts himself to the Lord."

Indeed, "these three attitudes displayed by David at a dark moment, a moment of testing, can help all of us" when we find ourselves in difficult situations. We mustn't "negotiate our position." We need to "accept penance," the pope repeated, to understand the reasons why we "need to do penance," and thus "weep for our mistakes, our sins." Last, we must not try to take the law into our own hands; we should "entrust ourselves to God."

Pope Francis concluded his homily by inviting us to invoke David, whom we "venerate as a saint," asking him to teach us to display "these attitudes at the dark moments of our lives." For each of us can be "someone who loves God, loves our people and doesn't trade them, someone who knows we're a sinner and does penance, someone who is sure of our God and trusts in him."

WHEN GOD CRIES

Tuesday, February 4, 2014
II SAMUEL 18:9-10, 14, 24-25, 30; 19:1-4; MARK 5:21-43

"Every good father needs his child: he waits for the child, loves, forgives, wants his child near him, as close as a hen wants her chicks." Pope Francis said this in his homily at the Mass celebrated on Tuesday morning, February 4, in the chapel of St. Martha's Guest House.

Commenting on the day's liturgical readings, the pope took the theme of fatherhood, relating it to the two main characters described in Mark's gospel (5:21-43) and in the second book of Samuel (18:9-10, 14, 24-25, 30; 19:1-4). These were Jairus, a leader of the synagogue in Jesus' time, "who goes to ask him to heal his daughter," and David, "who is suffering from the war his son is waging on him." Two events which, according to the bishop of Rome, show how for every father "his child is a blessing: he can't think of himself without the child."

The pope focused first on the king of Israel. He recalled that, although David's son Absalom had become his enemy, David "waited for news from the war. He sat between the two doors of the palace and kept watch." Although everyone was sure he was waiting for "news of a great victory," he was really "awaiting something else: his son. He was concerned about his son. He was king, ruler of the country but," first and foremost, "he was a father." So "when news came of his son's death," David was convulsed. He went up to the room over the gate and wept: "O my son Absalom, my son, my son Absalom. Would that I had died instead of you. O Absalom, my son, my son!"

"This," said Pope Francis, "is the heart of a father, who never rejects his son;" even though he "is a villain or an enemy," he weeps for him. The pope noted that David weeps twice in the Bible for his children: here he weeps for Absalom and he weeps again when the child he got by adultery is dying: "That time too he fasted and did penance to save his child's life," because "he was a father."

Going back to the story in the biblical passage, the bishop of Rome noted another feature of it: silence. "The soldiers returned from battle to the city in silence," he noted. Whereas when David was a young man, when he re-entered the city after killing the Philistine, all the women came out of their homes "to praise and acclaim him, because that's how soldiers were greeted after a victory." However, when Absalom dies, "the victory was covered up because the king was weeping." For "rather than being a king and conqueror," David was above all "a grieving father."

Turning to the character in the gospel, the leader of the synagogue, Pope Francis noted that he was "an important man," but "when his daughter became ill" he was not ashamed to throw himself at Jesus' feet and implore him: "My little girl is dying, come and lay your hands on her to save her so that she'll live!" This man doesn't think about the consequences of his action. He doesn't stop to think whether "if instead of being a prophet Christ was a sorcerer," whether he would risk losing face. "As a father," said the pope, "he doesn't stop to think, he takes the risk, he prostrates himself and pleads." At this scene too, when they go into the house they find weeping and wailing. "There were people

wailing loudly because that was their job; it was their job to wail
in houses of the dead." But this "wasn't the cry of a father."

So here we have two fathers. For each of them their priority
is their child. And that "makes us think of the first thing we say
about God in the Creed: 'I believe in God the father.' It makes
us think of God's fatherhood. That's how God is with us." But
someone might object: "But Father, God doesn't cry!" To which
the pope replied. "Of course he does! Remember when Jesus
wept over Jerusalem: 'Jerusalem, Jerusalem, how often have I
wanted to gather your children!' as a hen gathers her chicks under her wings!" So "God weeps; Jesus wept for us." And that
weeping is the cry of a father "who wants us all with him at
difficult times."

The pope then recalled that in the Bible there are at least "two
bad times when the father responds to the cry of his child. First,
there is the story of Isaac who is being led to his death by Abraham to be offered in sacrifice. Isaac realizes "they were carrying
the wood and the fire, but not the lamb for the sacrifice." So "his
heart was afraid. And what does he say? 'Father.' And the reply:
'Here I am, my son.'" The second time is "Jesus in the Garden
of Olives, with anguish in his heart: 'Father, if it is possible take
away this cup from me.' And angels came to give him strength.
That's what our God is like. He's a father."

The image of David waiting for news between the two doors
of his palace also calls to mind the parable in chapter 15 of Luke's
gospel, of the father waiting for the return of his prodigal son,
"who had gone off with all the money, his whole inheritance.
How do we know he was waiting for him?" asked Pope Francis.
"Because," he replied, and it's the answer given us in the biblical
story, "he saw him far off. And because every day he had been
waiting" for his son to return. In that loving father we see "our
God," who "is a father." Hence the hope that physical fatherhood
in families and the spiritual fatherhood of priests and bishops

should always be like that of the two main characters in these readings: "two men who are fathers."

In conclusion the pope invited us to meditate on these two "images": David weeping and the leader of the synagogue throwing himself at Jesus' feet without shame or fear of becoming ridiculous, because "their child was at stake." And the pope asked the faithful to renew their profession of faith, saying "I believe in God the Father" and to ask the Holy Spirit to teach us to say "Abba, Father." Because, he concluded, "it is a grace to be able to say 'Father' to God with our whole heart."

What We Leave to Others

Thursday, February 6, 2014
1 Kings 2:1-4, 10-12

We should live our whole life in the church as sinners but not as corrupt traitors. We should have an attitude of hope so that we leave a legacy which doesn't consist of material wealth but is a testimony of holiness. These were the "great graces" Pope Francis spoke about during the Mass celebrated on Thursday morning, February 6, in the chapel of St. Martha's Guest House.

The bishop of Rome focused his reflection on the mystery of death, beginning from the first reading—taken from the first book of Kings (2:1-4; 10-12)—in which, he said, "we heard the story of David's death." And "we remember the beginning of his life, when he was chosen by the Lord, anointed by the Lord." He was just "a young lad." Then "after a few years he began to reign," but he was always "a young man, he was twenty-two or twenty-three years old."

So David's whole life is "a course, a road traveled in the service of his people." And "he finished as he began." The same thing happens in our own lives, noted the pope. They "begin, progress, and end."

The story of David's death suggested three "heartfelt" thoughts to the pope. First, he remarked that "David dies inside the church, among his people. His death doesn't happen away from his people but "among" them. Thus "he belongs to the people of God." However, David "had sinned: he called himself a sinner." But "he never left the people of God: yes, he was a sinner, but not a traitor." This, said the pope, "is a grace": the grace of "remaining with the people of God till the end" and "dying in the bosom of the church, that is, in the bosom of the people of God."

Stressing this aspect, the pope invited us "to ask for the grace to die at home, within the church." He said, "This is a grace" which "can't be bought," because "it's a gift from God." We "must ask for it: Lord, give me the gift of dying at home, within the church." Although we are "all sinners," we mustn't become "traitors" or "corrupt."

The church, said the pope, "is our mother and wants us just as we are," although "we are often dirty." Because she's the one who "cleans us up: she's a mother, she knows how to." But it's up to us "to ask for this grace: to die at home, inside the church."

Pope Francis then offered a second reflection on David's death. "In this story," he noted, "we see that David is calm, at peace, serene." So "he calls his son and tells him: I'm about to go the way of all the earth." In other words David realizes: "Now it's my turn!" Then we read in the Bible: "David slept with his fathers." Here, explained the pope, we have the king "accepting his death in hope, in peace. This is another grace: the grace to die in hope," being "aware that it's just a step" and "we're awaited elsewhere." And indeed, after his death "the household continues, the family continues: I won't be alone!" It's a grace asked for especially "at life's final moments: we know life is a struggle and the spirit of evil wants his prey."

The bishop of Rome also recalled the testimony of St. Thérèse of the Child Jesus, who said that at the end of her life there was a struggle in her soul and when she thought about the future, about what awaited her after death, in heaven, she heard a sort of voice saying: no, don't be silly, what awaits you is darkness, all that awaits you is the darkness of nothing!" That, said the pope, "was the devil who didn't want her to entrust herself to God."

Hence the importance of "asking for the grace of dying in hope and trusting in God." But "trusting in God," he stressed, "begins now, both in life's little things and big problems: always entrust ourselves to the Lord. Thus we get into the habit of trusting in the Lord and so our hope grows." So, he explained, "dying at home, in hope" are "two things David's death teaches us."

The third thought suggested by the pope was "the problem of inheritance." And by the way, he pointed out, "the Bible doesn't tell us that when David died all his grandchildren and great-grandchildren came to demand their inheritance!" There are often "so many scandals caused by inheritance, so many scandals that set families at war." But the legacy David leaves isn't wealth. The Bible tells us that "his kingdom grew stronger and stronger": David "left a legacy of a forty-year reign for his people, who grew stronger and stronger."

Here the pope recalled a popular saying, that "in their lifetime everyone should have a child, plant a tree and write a book: that's the best legacy." The pope invited each of us to ask ourselves: "What legacy will I leave to those who come after me? A legacy of life? Have I done the good required of me as a father or mother?" Maybe "I haven't planted a tree" or "written a book," but "have I given life, wisdom?" A "true legacy is like David's," when on his deathbed he tells his son Solomon: "Be strong and courageous. Keep the charge of the Lord your God, walking in his ways and keeping his statutes."

David's words help us understand that the real "legacy is our witness as Christians that we leave to others." Indeed, there are some who "leave a great legacy: think of the saints who lived by the gospel so forcefully." They "leave us a way of life, a way of living as their legacy."

In conclusion, the pope repeated the three points of his reflection and turned them into a prayer to St. David, to "give all of us these three graces: to ask for the grace to die at home, to die in the church; ask for the grace to die in hope, with hope; and ask for the grace to leave behind a good legacy, a human legacy, a legacy that is the witness of our Christian life."

BACK TO THAT FIRST MEETING IN GALILEE

Friday, February 7, 2014
MARK 6:14-29

Jesus must be proclaimed and confessed with power and clarity, without half measures. We must always go back to the "first meeting" with him and also be able to bear "the soul's dark times." The "model disciple" described by Pope Francis is represented by the figure of John the Baptist. And it was on the precursor of Jesus that Pope Francis focused his meditation during the Mass celebrated on Friday, February 7, in St. Martha's House in the Vatican.

Taking his cue from the story of his preaching and death, as told in the gospel of Mark (6:14-29), the pope said that John is "a man who had a short lifetime, a short lifetime in which to proclaim God's word." He was "the man sent by God to prepare the way for his Son."

But "John ends badly." He is beheaded by order of Herod. He becomes "the price of an entertainment for the royal court at a banquet." And, commented the pope, "when it's the court anything can be done: corruption, vice, crime. Courts encourage these things."

So the pope described the figure of John the Baptist, pointing out three fundamental features. "What did John do? First of all," he explained, "he proclaimed the Lord. He proclaimed that the Savior, the Lord was near; the kingdom of God was at hand." A proclamation he "made forcefully: he baptized and urged all to repent." John was "a powerful man and he proclaimed Jesus Christ: he was the prophet nearest to Jesus Christ. He was so close that he himself pointed him out." Indeed, when he saw Jesus, he exclaimed: "He's the one!"

The second feature of his witness, explained he pope, "is that he doesn't exploit his moral authority," even though "the chance to say 'I'm the Messiah'" was offered to him "on a plate!" In fact, John "had so much moral authority, such a lot! All the people were flocking to him. The gospel tells us that the scribes" were going to him to ask him, "What must we do?" So were the people and the soldiers. "Repent!" was John's reply and "don't swindle people!"

"The Pharisees and doctors" also looked to John's "power," recognizing that he was "an upright man. That's why they went to ask him: are you the Messiah?" For John that was "the moment of temptation to vanity." He could have answered: "I can't speak about this . . ." and "left the question up in the air. Or he could have said: 'I don't know . . .' with false humility." Instead, John "speaks out plainly" and declares: "No, I'm not! The one who is more powerful than me is coming after me; I'm not worthy to stoop down and untie the thong of his sandals."

So he didn't fall into the temptation of hogging "the title, he didn't grab the honor." He said plainly: "I am a voice, just that. The word comes after me. I am a voice!" And "that," said the pope, "is the second thing John did: he didn't grab the honor." He was "a truthful man."

"The third thing John did," continued the pope, "was to imitate Christ, imitate Jesus. To the point where in those days, the scribes and doctors thought that he was the Messiah." Even "Herod, who had killed John, believed that Jesus was John." That shows how closely the Baptist had "followed the way of Jesus, especially the way of humility."

Indeed, "John humbled himself, humbled himself to the end, to the death." He met "the same shameful death" as the Lord: "Jesus as a villain, a thief, a criminal, on the cross" and John as the victim of "a weak and lecherous man," who goes along with "the hatred of an adulteress and the whim of a dancer." These are two "humiliating deaths."

Like Jesus, continued the pope, "John also had his Gethsemane, his anguish in prison when he thought he had been mistaken." So "he sends his disciples to ask Jesus: Tell me, are you the one, or have I made a mistake and it's someone else?" That's the experience of "darkness in the soul," a "darkness that purifies." Jesus answered John as the Father answered Jesus: by giving him strength.

Speaking of "the darkness of a man of God or woman of God," Pope Francis recalled the witness "of blessed Teresa of Calcutta. The woman whom the whole world praised, the Nobel Prize winner! But she knew that at one time in her life, a long time, there was only darkness within her." And "John also suffered that darkness," but he was "the proclaimer of Jesus Christ; he didn't exploit the prophecy for himself" but became "an imitator of Jesus Christ."

So in John we find the "model" and "the vocation of a disciple." The "source of this behavior" can be found in the gospel story of Mary's visit to Elizabeth, when "John danced for joy in his mother's womb." In fact, Jesus and John "were cousins" and "perhaps they met later." But that first "meeting filled John's heart with joy, such great joy. And it turned him into a disciple," into "the man who proclaimed Jesus Christ, who did not take over the place of Jesus Christ, but followed the way of Jesus Christ."

In conclusion Pope Francis suggested an examination of conscience "on our discipleship," by asking ourselves a few questions: "Do we proclaim Jesus Christ? Do we or don't we take advantage of our being Christians as if it were a privilege?" Here it's important to look to the example John, who "doesn't take advantage of the prophecy."

A further question: "Do we go the way of Jesus Christ, the way of humiliation, humility, humbling ourselves in order to serve?"

If we realize "we are not steadfast in this," said the pope, it's good to "ask ourselves: when was my meeting with Jesus Christ, that meeting which filled me with joy?" It's a way of going back to that first meeting with the Lord, "back to that first meeting in Galilee: we've all had one!" The secret, said the pope, is to "go back there: meet the Lord and then go forward along that beautiful way, in which he must increase and we must decrease."

No Clock Watching at Mass

Monday, February 10, 2014
1 Kings 8:1-7, 9-13

You don't go to Mass carrying a clock, as if you had to count the minutes you spend attending a performance. You go to share in God's mystery. That's also true for all who attend the Mass at St. Martha's celebrated by the pope. The pope said this morning, Monday, February 10, to the faithful present in the chapel of the house where he lives: "It's not a tourist attraction. No! You come here and we gather to enter into the mystery. That's the liturgy."

To explain the meaning of this encounter with the mystery, Pope Francis recalled that the Lord didn't only speak to his people with words. "The prophets," he said, "related the words of the Lord. The prophets proclaimed them. The great prophet Moses gave the commandments, which are the words of the Lord. And so many other prophets told the people what the Lord wanted." However, he added, "the Lord also spoke to his people in other ways and in another form: by theophanies. So when he approaches the people, he makes himself felt, he makes his presence felt among the people." Besides the episode described in the first reading (1 Kings 8:1-7, 9-13), the pope recalled other passages referring to other prophets.

"The same thing happens in church," the pope explained. The Lord speaks to us through his word, collected in the gospel and the Bible, and through catechesis, and homilies. Not only does he speak to us, he said, "but he also becomes present among his people, in the midst of his church. It's the presence of the Lord. The Lord comes close to his people; he becomes present and spends a bit of time with his people."

That's what happens during the celebration of the liturgy, which is certainly not "a social occasion," the bishop of Rome continued, "neither is it a gathering of believers to pray together. It's something else," because "in the liturgy of the Eucharist God is present," and, if that's possible, he's present even "more intimately." And the pope repeated "it's a real presence."

The pope went on to say, "when I speak of the liturgy, I'm referring mainly to Holy Mass. When we celebrate Mass, we are not creating a representation of the Last Supper." Mass "isn't a representation; it's something else. It *is* the Last Supper; it's actually reliving once more the Lord's passion and redeeming death. It's a theophany: the Lord becomes present on the altar to be offered to the Father for the salvation of the world."

Then, as he often does, Pope Francis described a common practice by the faithful: "We feel or we say, 'I can't do that now, I've got to go to Mass, I've got to go and hear Mass.' But Mass isn't for listening to: it's for taking part in. We take part in this theophany, this mystery of the Lord's presence among us." It's something different from our other forms of devotion, he said and cited the example of the "living crib," "which we have in our parishes at Christmas, or the Stations of the Cross we make during Holy Week." These, he explained, are representations; the Eucharist is "a real commemoration, that is, it's a theophany. God comes close, is with us, and we share in the mystery of redemption."

Then the pope referred to another quite common way of behaving among Christians: "How often," he noted, "do we count the minutes . . . 'I've got just half an hour, I've got to go to Mass . . .'" That "isn't the right behavior required of us by the liturgy: the liturgy is God's time and God's space, and when we enter God's time and God's space, we shouldn't keep looking at our watch. The liturgy is entering into God's mystery, letting the mystery take us over, and being in the mystery."

Turning to those present at the celebration he continued: "For example, I'm sure that all of you have come to enter into the mystery. But perhaps someone has said, 'I must go to Mass at St. Martha's, because it's part of the tourist trip to go and visit the pope at St. Martha's every morning . . .' No! You come here, we gather here to enter into the mystery. And this is the liturgy, God's time, God's space, God's cloud enveloping us all."

So then Pope Francis shared some memories of his childhood with those present: "I remember when I was a child and we were preparing for our first communion, they got us to sing 'O holy altar guarded by angels,' and that led us to understand that the altar was guarded by angels, it gave us the sense of God's glory. And then, when they rehearsed us for the communion, they brought the hosts to show us and said: 'Look, these are not the ones you will receive: these aren't worth anything, because they haven't been consecrated.' They made us see the difference between the one and the other, between the reminder and the true commemoration." So celebrating the liturgy means "being ready to enter God's mystery," his space, his time.

In conclusion, the pope invited those present to "ask the Lord today to give all of us that sense of the sacred, that sense to realize that it's one thing to pray at home, pray in church, pray the rosary, pray so many fine prayers, make the Stations of the Cross, read the Bible; it's quite another to celebrate the Eucharist. During the celebration we enter into God's mystery, we go along with something we can't control: he's the only one, he's the glory, he's the power. Let us ask for the grace that the Lord may teach us to enter into God's mystery."

The King and the Woman

Thursday, February 13, 2014
1 Kings 11:4-13; Mark 7:24-30

"Two figures" to illustrate one truth. We may be sinners but not corrupt. Pope Francis warned against the risk of corruption at the Mass celebrated on Thursday morning, February 13, in the chapel of St. Martha's Guest House. He pointed to two emblematic figures in the Bible—King Solomon and the woman who asks Jesus to intervene and cure her daughter possessed by a demon. The pope wanted to encourage those who silently seek the Lord every day, passing from idolatry to true faith.

The "two figures" chosen by the pope for his homily were taken from the day's liturgy. In the first book of Kings (11:4-13) we have the story of Solomon, and Mark's gospel (7:24-30) gives us the story of the woman, "who was Syro-Phoenician and spoke Greek," who begs Jesus "to drive the demon out of her daughter." Solomon and this woman, the pope explained, follow two opposite ways and through them "the church asks us to reflect on the road from paganism and idolatry to the living God, and from the living God toward idolatry."

We read in the gospel passage that in turning to Jesus this woman was "brave," as is every "desperate mother" seeking "the health of her child," and she's ready to do anything. "She'd been told that Jesus was a good man, a prophet," explained the pope, and so she went to find him, even though she "didn't believe in the God of Israel." For the good of her daughter "she wasn't ashamed of the looks the apostles gave her." For "perhaps they were saying to one another: what's this Gentile woman doing here?" She approaches Jesus to beg him to help her daughter possessed by an unclean spirit. But Jesus replies that he has "come first for the lost sheep of the house of Israel." He "tells her in harsh words: 'Let the children be fed first, for it is not right to take the children's bread and throw it to the dogs.'"

The woman, who "certainly hadn't been to university," noted the Holy Father, didn't answer Jesus "with her mind but with her mother's instinct, with her love." So she said to him: "Yet even the dogs under the table eat the children's crumbs." As if to say: "Give me those crumbs!" Struck by her faith, "the Lord worked a miracle." Then when she "got home, she found her little girl lying in bed and the demon had left her."

This, in substance, is the story of a mother who "risked looking foolish but persisted" out of love for her daughter. Though coming "from paganism and idolatry, she won health for her daughter." And she herself "found the living God." That, explained the pope, "is the way of a person of good will who seeks God and finds him." Because of her faith "the Lord blesses her." But it's also the story of so many people who "make this journey" today. And "the Lord is waiting" for these people moved by the Holy Spirit. "Every day in the Lord's church there are people who make this journey, silently, to find the Lord," because "they allow themselves to be led by the Holy Spirit."

But, the pope warned, there is also "the opposite way," represented by the figure of Solomon, "the wisest man on Earth, with a heap of great, enormous blessings; inheriting a united country, a union achieved by his father David." King Solomon was "universally famous," he had "all power." And he was also "a believer in God." So why did he lose his faith? We find the answer in the biblical passage: "His women turned away his heart after other gods; and his heart was not wholly true to the Lord his God, as was the heart of David his father."

"Solomon liked women," said the pope. "He had so many concubines and he got them from all over the place: each had her god, her idol." It was "these women who gradually weakened Solomon's heart." So Solomon "lost the integrity" of his faith. Then when "one woman asked him for a little temple" for "her god," he built one "on the mountain." And when another woman asked him for incense for her idol, he bought some for her. But in doing so, "his heart was weakened and he lost his faith."

So, remarked the pope, "the wisest man in the world" let himself be corrupted "through unwise love, without discretion, through his passions." However, said the pope, you could reply: "But Father, Solomon didn't lose his faith; he believed in God, he could recite the Bible" by heart. But the pope answered that objection: "Having faith doesn't mean being able to recite the Creed: you can recite the Creed and still have lost your faith!"

"At first," the pope continued, "Solomon was a sinner like his father David. But then he persisted in his sin" and became "corrupt: his heart was corrupted by that idolatry." His father David "was also a sinner, but the Lord forgave all his sins because he was humble and asked for forgiveness." On the other hand, "vanity and his passions led" Solomon "to corruption." For "it's in our hearts that faith is lost."

So the king "goes the opposite way to that of the Syro-Phoenician woman: she from pagan idolatry comes to the living God," but he "goes from the living God to pagan idolatry: poor man! She was a sinner, certainly, because we all are. But he was corrupt."

Quoting the Letter to the Hebrews, the pope hoped that "no bad seed might grow" in our hearts. It was "the bad seed of passions that grew in Solomon's heart," and "led him to idolatry." To stop that seed from growing the bishop of Rome pointed to "the good advice," suggested by the liturgy in the gospel acclamation: "Humbly welcome the word that has been planted in you and can bring you to salvation." With that awareness, he concluded, "let us go the way of the Canaanite woman, that Gentile woman, welcoming God's word that has been planted in us and which will lead to salvation." May God's own word which is "strong, keep us on this way and not let us end up in corruption following the way that leads us to idolatry."

Getting Over the Obstacles

Friday, February 14, 2014
Acts 13:46-49; Mark 7:31-37

Carrying on, getting over the obstacles—that's the right attitude for good Christians because it's part of their identity. So a Christian who doesn't carry on, who doesn't go ahead be-

yond the obstacles, has "identity sickness." During the Mass celebrated on Friday morning, February 14, Pope Francis repeated
the invitation he often gives to the faithful he meets: "Go ahead,
carry on." In doing so he recalled two brothers who are patrons of
Europe, Cyril and Methodius, whose feast day it was. As disciples
they were sent into the world to bring the message, and their
progress, the pope stressed, "leads us to reflect on the identity of
a disciple," that is, Christian identity.

But, asked the pope, "who is a Christian?" "How does a Christian behave?" His answer was: the Christian "is a disciple. A disciple who is sent out. The gospel is clear: the Lord sends them
out, go, go ahead! And that means a Christian is a disciple of the
Lord who is on the move, who always carries on. We can't imagine a static Christian, a Christian who stays still, with a feeble
Christian identity." Recalling what had just been proclaimed in
the psalm, the pope repeated that a Christian is a disciple who
goes ahead, who carries on: "Go into all the world and proclaim
the gospel" (Mk 16:15).

However, for the Christian, going ahead also means "getting
over the difficulties." To explain this statement Pope Francis referred to the day's reading taken from the Acts of the Apostles
(13:46-49), in which, when they were in Pisidian Antioch, Paul
and Barnabas saw that the Jews were not following them, so they
"went to the Gentiles. Go ahead!" And, the pope continued, in
the parable of the wedding feast, Jesus "also did the same. The invited guests didn't turn up; they all found an excuse not to come.
So what does Jesus say? Shall we cancel the party? No! 'Go out
to the crossroads and streets and invite everyone, good and bad.'
That's what the gospel tells us. But invite the bad people as well?
Yes, them too! Everyone! Christians go ahead; if there are difficulties, they get over them to proclaim that the kingdom of God
is near."

The second feature of Christian identity is that "we must

always stay as lambs. An ancient paschal antiphon has us sing: 'These are the newly baptized lambs.'" Pope Francis referred to the passage from Luke's gospel (10:1-9): 'Go on your way. See I'm sending you out like lambs among wolves.'" David, recalled the pope, didn't accept the armor offered to him to fight the Philistine: he wouldn't have been able to move, he wouldn't have been "himself, the humble, simple David. In the end he just took a sling and won the battle." We must stay as lambs and "not become wolves, because sometimes," said the Holy Father, "there's the temptation to think: 'This is difficult, these wolves are cunning and I'll be even more cunning than them!'" So remain as "lambs, not daft, but still lambs. Lambs with Christian shrewdness, but still lambs. Because if you're a lamb God will defend you. But if you feel you're strong as a wolf God won't defend you, but leave you on your own. The wolves will gobble you up."

So, he asked, "what is the characteristic of this lamblike Christian?" The pope then mentioned the third element in Christian identity: "Joy," was his answer. He continued: "Isaiah tells us in his book (52:7): How beautiful upon the mountains are the feet of the messenger who announces peace, who comes to tell us that the Lord is king. They're people who rejoice because they know the Lord and bring the Lord." For: "Joy is the style of the Christian. A Christian can't go about without joy. You can't go about like lambs without joy." We must keep this attitude even when faced with problems, in difficult times, even "in the face of our own mistakes and sins," because "it's the joy of Jesus who always forgives and helps us."

So, the bishop of Rome repeated, the gospel must be brought to the world by these lambs who go about it with joy. Then he warned: "Those Christians aren't doing the Lord any favors in the church whose tempo is *adagio lamentoso*, who always behave like that, complaining about everything, being miserable. That's not the style of a disciple. St. Augustine says: go, go ahead, sing and carry on, with joy! That's the style of a Christian: to proclaim the gospel with joy." Whereas "being miserable and even bitter lead us to practice a so-called Christianity without Christ." Christians are never still: they're men and women who always carry on, who get over the difficulties. They do so with their strength and their joy. He concluded: "May the Lord grant us the grace to live like Christians who go about joyfully like lambs."

HOLY PATIENCE

Monday, February 17, 2014
JAMES 1:1-11; MARK 8:11-13

There are people who suffer with a smile and keep "the joy of faith" despite trials and illnesses. These are the people who "carry the church forward by their everyday holiness," so that they become real beacons "in our parishes, our institutions." This was Pope Francis' reflection on "the exemplary patience of the people of God," which he gave on Monday, February 17, during the Mass in the chapel of St. Martha's Guest House. It contained echoes of his meeting, on the previous Sunday afternoon, with the parish community on the outskirts of Rome called Infernetto.

"When we go to the parishes," said the bishop of Rome, "we meet people who are suffering, who have problems, who have a disabled child or are ill, but they carry on living patiently." These people "don't ask for a miracle" but live "with God's patience," reading "the signs of the times." And "the world is unworthy" of these holy people of God, declared the pope, quoting chapter 11 of the Letter to the Hebrews. "We can also say about these people of ours—people who suffer, suffer so much, from so many things but never lose their smile, who keep the joy of faith—that the world isn't worthy of them: it's unworthy! The spirit of the world is unworthy of such people!"

The pope's reflection on the value of patience took its cue, as usual, from the day's liturgy: the passage from the Letter of James (1:1-11) and from Mark's gospel (8:11-13).

"Count it all joy, my brothers, when you meet various trials." Commenting on these words taken from the first reading, the pope noted that "what the apostle James says seems rather strange." It almost seems like "an invitation to act like a fakir." For, he asked, "how can we enjoy undergoing a trial?" The pope continued with the reading of the passage from St. James: "For you know that the testing of your faith produces patience. And let patience have its full effect, that you may be perfect and complete, lacking in nothing."

This, he explained, is suggesting that we "lead our lives according to the rhythm of patience." But, he pointed out, "patience isn't resignation, it's something else." Actually, patience means "carrying life's burdens on our shoulders, things that aren't good, horrible things, things we don't want. That patience is what will make our lives become mature." Someone without patience "wants everything at once, everything in a hurry." And "someone who doesn't have the wisdom of patience is a willful person," who ends up acting "like a willful child," who says, "I want this, I want that, I don't like this," and is never happy with anything.

"Why does this generation ask for a sign?" asks the Lord in the gospel passage from Mark, in reply to a request from the Pharisees. What he meant, said the pope, was that "this generation is like children who hear happy music and won't dance and sad music and won't cry. Nothing is right for them!" Indeed, the pope continued, "someone without patience is someone who doesn't grow, who remains a willful child, who can't take life as it comes," and can only say: "Either that or nothing!"

Where there is no patience, "one of the temptations is to become willful" like children. Another temptation of those "who lack patience is wanting to be omnipotent. They demand: 'I want this now!'" That's what the Lord is referring to when the Pharisees ask him for "a sign from heaven." For really, said the pope, "what did they want? They wanted a spectacle, a miracle." Actually, it's the same temptation as the one the devil proposed to Jesus in the wilderness; he urged him to do something—turn these stones into bread and everyone will believe in you—or throw yourself down from the temple to show your power.

But, in asking Jesus for a sign, the Pharisees "confuse God's way of working with that of a sorcerer. God has his own way of doing things: God's patience." And "every time we go to the sacrament of reconciliation, we sing a hymn to God's patience. The Lord carries us on his back, so patiently!"

"Christian life," suggested the pope, "must dance to that music of patience, because it was the music of our fathers: the people of God, who followed the commandment the Lord gave to our father Abraham: walk on and be blameless!"

The people, he continued, still quoting chapter 11 of the Letter to the Hebrews, "have suffered so much: they've been persecuted, killed, they had to hide in caves and caverns. And they were glad, joyful—as the apostle James says—to greet the promises from afar." That's the patience we must have during trials. It's "the patience of a grown-up person, God's patience who bears with us, carries us on his back; it's the patience of our people," said the pope and exclaimed: "How patient our people are even now!"

Thus the bishop of Rome recalled that there are so many suffering people who "carry on their lives with patience. They don't ask for a sign," like the Pharisees, "but they know how to read the signs of the times." So "they know when the fig tree sprouts spring is coming." But the "impatient people," described in the gospel, "wanted a sign" but "they didn't know how to read the signs of the times. That's why they didn't recognize Jesus."

The Letter to the Hebrews, said the pope, says clearly that "the world was unworthy of the people of God." But today "we can say the same about those among our people: those who suffer, suffer so much, from so many things but never lose their smile, keep the joy of faith." Yes, "the world isn't worthy" of them either! It's "these people, our people, in our parishes, in our institutions," who "carry the church forward by their everyday holiness, every day."

In conclusion, the pope reread the passage from St. James he had referred to at the beginning of his homily. He asked the Lord to give "all of us patience: joyful patience, patience to work, patience of peace," giving us "God's patience" and "the patience of our faithful people which is so exemplary.

Avoid Falling into Temptation

Tuesday, February 18, 2014
James: 1:12-18; Mark 8:14-21

Temptation presents itself to us in a crafty way; it contaminates the atmosphere around us and always drives us to look for a justification. Finally, it makes us fall into sin, shutting us up in a cage from which it's difficult to escape. To resist it we must listen to the word of the Lord, because "he's waiting for us," he always gives us confidence and opens a new horizon before us. That, in brief, was the substance of Pope Francis' reflection during the Mass celebrated at St. Martha's this morning, Tuesday, February 18.

As usual, the pope took his cue from the day's liturgy, in particular from the Letter of St. James (1:12-18) in which, after having spoken to us about patience, the apostle speaks to us today about resistance. Resistance to temptations. He explains that each of us is tempted by our own passions, which lure us and seduce us. Then these passions conceive and give birth to sin. And once committed, sin gives birth to death.

But where does temptation come from? The pope turned again to the text of James's Letter. "The apostle," he observed, "tells us that temptation doesn't come from God, but from our passions, our inner weaknesses, the damage that original sin has left in us. That's where temptations come from." He went on to describe the characteristics of temptation, which, he said, "grows, contaminates, and justifies itself."

So at first, temptation "begins quietly," but "then it grows. Jesus himself said so in the parable of the good seed and the weeds (Matthew 13:24-30). The good seed grew, but the weeds that his enemy had sown also grew. That's how temptation grows, and grows, and grows. And if you don't check it, it takes over everything." Then comes the contamination. Temptation "grows, but," the bishop of Rome explained, "it doesn't like being alone." So "it seeks for another to keep it company; it contaminates someone else and thus it accumulates people." And the third characteristic is self-justification, because we humans "justify ourselves in order to feel all right."

The pope then observed that temptation has always justified itself "since the original sin," when Adam blames Eve for persuading him to eat the forbidden fruit. That's how it grows, contaminates, and justifies itself, then "it locks us in an environment from which we can't easily escape." In order to explain, the pope referred to the passage from Mark's gospel (8:14-21): "It's what happened to the apostles when they were in the boat. They had forgotten to bring bread," and they began arguing and blaming one another for forgetting it. Jesus looked at them. And he said to them: "Remember the yeast of the Pharisees and the yeast of

Herod? Watch out! Beware of it." However, "they didn't understand at all, because they were so caught up in blaming one another that they couldn't think about anything else; they had no light to grasp God's word."

The same thing happens "when we fall into temptation. We don't hear God's word. We don't get it. Jesus reminded the disciples of the multiplication of the loaves to help them get out of that impasse." That happens, explained the pope, because temptation closes off every horizon from "and leads us to sin." When we are being tempted, "only God's word, the word of Jesus, can save us. Hearing that word opens the horizon for us," because "he's always ready to teach us how to escape from temptation. Jesus is great not only because he enables us to escape from temptation but because he gives us more confidence."

Then Pope Francis recalled the episode in Luke's gospel (22:31-32), the conversation in which the Lord "says to Peter that the devil wanted to sift him like wheat." But at the same time he tells him that he has prayed for him and he gives Peter a new mission: "When once you have turned again, strengthen your brothers." So, the Holy Father stressed, Jesus not only awaits us in order to help us escape from temptation, but he trusts us. And "that's a great strength," because "he always opens new horizons for us," whereas, through temptation, the devil "closes them off and promotes an atmosphere of quarreling," so that "people try to justify themselves and accuse one another."

"Let's not allow ourselves to be imprisoned by temptation," urged the bishop of Rome. From the closed circle temptation traps us in "we can only escape by listening to the word of Jesus." He concluded: "Let us ask the Lord, that whenever we are being tempted he may say to us patiently, as he did to the disciples: 'Stop. Keep still. Raise your eyes and look toward the horizon. Don't be shut in. Go ahead.' That word will save us from falling into sin when we are tempted."

BUT WHO DO YOU SAY THAT I AM?

Thursday, February 20, 2014
MARK 8:27-33

"But who do you say that I am?" The question Jesus asks his disciples is put to each one of us two thousand years on, and requires an answer. An answer not to be found in books as a formula but in the experience of anyone who really follows Jesus, with the help of that "great worker," the Holy Spirit. That was the description of a disciple given by Pope Francis at the Mass celebrated on Thursday morning, February 20, in the chapel of St. Martha's Guest House.

At the heart of the Pope's meditation we have Peter, as he is presented in the gospel passage from Mark (8:27-33). It was Peter, the pope explained, "who was certainly the bravest on that day. When Jesus asked the disciples: 'But who do you say that I am?' Peter replied decisively: 'You are the Christ.'" After that confession, the pope remarked, he probably "felt satisfied within himself: 'I said the right thing!'" And truly "he did say the right thing."

But the conversation with Jesus doesn't end there. Indeed, said the pope, "the Lord began to explain what had to happen." But Peter didn't agree with what he was hearing: "he didn't like the prospect" of what Jesus was telling them. The gospel tells us, "he was telling them openly."

Today too, the bishop of Rome continued, "we hear so often within ourselves" the same question Jesus put to the apostles. Jesus turns to us and asks us: but for you who am I? Who is Jesus Christ for each one of us, for me? Who is Jesus Christ? And, the pope noted, "we would surely give the same answer as Peter, which we learned in the catechism: you are the Son of the living God, you are the redeemer, you are the Lord!"

Peter's reaction was different "when Jesus began to explain

what had to happen: the son of man must suffer greatly and be rejected by the elders, the chief priests, and scribes and be killed, and after three days, rise again." Peter, said the pope, "certainly didn't like what he was hearing." He reasoned thus: "You are the Christ! You conquer and we go ahead!" So "he didn't understand that way" of suffering Jesus was pointing out. So, the gospel tells us that "he took him aside" and "began to rebuke him." He was "so pleased to have given that answer—'you are the Christ'—that he felt able to rebuke Jesus."

Pope Francis then read again what Jesus said word for word: "But turning and looking at his disciples, he rebuked Peter and said, 'Get behind me, Satan! For you are setting your mind not on divine things but on human things.'"

So in order to "reply to that question we all hear in our hearts— who is Jesus for us?—it's not enough to repeat what we've learned, studied in the catechism." Of course it's "important to study the catechism and to get to know it, but it isn't enough," insisted the Holy Father. Because to know him truly "it's necessary to make the journey Peter made." Indeed, "after that humiliation, Peter carried on with Jesus, he saw the miracles Jesus did, he saw his powers. Then he paid the taxes, as Jesus had told him to; he caught a fish and got the coin: he saw so many miracles of that kind!"

But "at a certain point Peter denied Jesus, he betrayed Jesus." At that very moment "he learned that difficult knowledge—wisdom rather than knowledge—of tears, of weeping." Peter asked the Lord "for forgiveness."

Then "in the uncertainty of that Easter Sunday morning, Peter didn't know what to think" about what the women had told him of the empty tomb. So he too "went to the tomb." The gospel doesn't tell us "the exact moment, but we're told that the Lord met Peter"; we're told that Peter "met the living Lord, alone, face to face."

Continuing with the story of Peter's journey, the pope remarked that, during the forty days that followed, Peter "heard so many explanations from Jesus about the kingdom of God. And perhaps he was tempted to think: ah, now I know who Jesus Christ is!" But he was still "missing many things to understand who Jesus was."

Then "that morning on the beach by the Sea of Tiberias, Peter was questioned again three times. He felt ashamed; he remembered that evening of Holy Thursday when he had denied Jesus three times." He remembered "that weeping." According to the pope, "on shore of the Sea of Tiberias Peter wept again, not bitterly as on that Thursday, but he did weep." The pope said he was "certain" that when Peter declared "Lord, you know everything, you know that I love you," he was weeping.

So "the question to Peter—who am I for you?—can only be understood by making a long journey, after a long journey. A journey of grace and sin." And "the journey of a disciple." For "Jesus didn't say to Peter or his other apostles: Know me! He said: Follow me!" And "it's by following Jesus that we get to know Jesus. Following Jesus with our virtues" and "also with our sins. But always following Jesus!"

To know Jesus, the Holy Father repeated, "it isn't necessary to study ideas, but to live as a disciple." In that way, "by walking with Jesus we learn who he is, we learn the knowledge of Jesus. We get to know Jesus as his disciples." We get to know him by "meeting daily with the Lord, every day. With our victories and our weaknesses." It's through "those meetings" that "we come close to him and get to know him more deeply." Because "in those everyday meetings we get what Paul calls the mind of Christ, the hermeneutics by which to judge everything."

But it's "a journey we can't make on our own," said the pope. He recalled that in Matthew's account of the episode (16:13-28), "when Peter confesses to Jesus you are the Son of God, the

Christ, Jesus tells him: you didn't learn that from human knowledge but the Father revealed it to you." Then again, "Jesus tells his disciples, 'the Holy Spirit, whom I will send you, will teach you all things and will make you understand what I have taught you.'"

So we get to know Jesus "as disciples on the road of life, by following him." But that "isn't enough," warned the pope, because "knowing Jesus is a gift from the Father: it is he who enables us to know Jesus." Really, he said, it's "a work of the Holy Spirit, who is the great worker: he's not a trade union official, he's a great worker. And he's always working in us and he does that great work of explaining the mystery of Jesus and giving us the mind of Christ."

The pope concluded his meditation by repeating Jesus' question: who am I for you? "As his disciples," he suggested, "let us ask the Father to give us the knowledge of Christ" and "the Holy Spirit to explain this mystery to us."

Faith Isn't Casuistry

Friday, February 21, 2014
James 2:14-24, 26

Asking what the church can or can't do, or what is or isn't allowed, is falling into casuistry which, together with ideology, is the sign by which to recognize someone who knows doctrine and theology by heart but lacks faith. For faith is never abstract: it must be a witness.

Pope Francis warned against the risk of faith without works this morning, Friday, February 21, during the Mass celebrated in the chapel of St. Martha's Guest House. The pope took his cue from the passage taken from the Letter of St. James (2:14-24, 26), which says that just as the body without the spirit is dead, so faith without works is dead. "The apostle James," explained the pope, "gives this teaching, which is an exhortation about faith." In order to do so, "he opposes faith and works." What James is saying "is clear: faith that doesn't bear fruit in works isn't faith."

"We too," warned the pope, "often make a mistake about this." We "hear someone saying: I have so much faith!" or "I believe everything!" but "perhaps the person saying this lives a lukewarm, feeble life." So "their faith is just a theory, not a living force in their life."

In his letter, the pope continued, "when the apostle James speaks about faith, he's talking about doctrine, the content of faith." And it's as if he were saying to each one of us: "But you can know all the commandments, all the prophecies, all the truths of faith but if all that" isn't translated "into practice, into works, it's no good."

So, said the pope, "theoretically we can even recite the Creed without faith. There are so many people who do that! Even the demons!" Actually, he added, "the demons know very well what is said in the Creed and know that it's true. 'They shudder,' says the apostle James, because they know it's true," even though they don't have faith. Demons "know all theology, they know Denzinger by heart," the classic manual containing the church's doctrinal formulations, "but they don't have faith." For, the pope declared, "having faith doesn't mean having knowledge: having faith means accepting God's message brought to us by Jesus Christ, living by it and carrying it out."

So Pope Francis gave "the signs" by which to recognize "someone who knows what we're supposed to believe but who doesn't have faith." The pope mentioned two in particular, which are found in the gospel. The first sign showing knowledge of theology without faith "is casuistry." He recalled all those who went to Jesus with casuistical questions, such as: "Is it lawful to pay taxes to Caesar?" Or the case of "that poor woman who had been widowed and, according to the Levitical law, she had to marry each of her husband's seven brothers in order to bear a child." That's "casuistry." And "casuistry," said the pope, "is where all those people go who think they have faith," but know only the content of faith. So "when we find Christians" who merely ask "whether it's lawful to do this or whether the church could do that," it means that "either they don't have faith or it's too weak."

The second sign pointed out by the pope was ideology. He said we can't be "Christians who think of the faith as a system of ideas, an ideology." That's a risk which "was also present in Jesus' time" and represented by the Gnostics. "The apostle James says of these ideologists of the faith that they're the Antichrist." So, the pope explained, those "who fall into casuistry or ideology are Christians who know the doctrine but lack faith. Like the demons. With the difference that the demons shudder, but these people don't: they live peacefully."

Pope Francis suggested three particular figures, taken from the gospel, who "don't know the doctrine but have great faith." He spoke about the Canaanite woman, a Gentile who had faith in Jesus, "because the Holy Spirit had touched her heart." She then "bore witness to her faith: that's the key." Then he mentioned the Samaritan woman, who "at first didn't believe in anything" or believed mistakenly, but who had "faith after her meeting with Jesus." That is, at first she had "a casuistic way of thinking," asking whether God should be worshiped "on this mountain or that," but after she had "spoken with the Lord, she felt something" in her heart and she "ran home to say: I've met someone who told me everything I ever did!" She had faith "because she had met Jesus Christ and not just an abstract truth."

The third figure from the gospel suggested by the pope was that of "the man born blind, who went to Jesus to ask for the gift of sight." Then, he added, "the poor man became involved in a quarrel between the Pharisees, Sadducees, and the doctors of the law: he and his parents were called to give evidence after that acrimonious dispute." The gospel tells us that "the Lord looked at him and asked him: 'Do you believe?'" That man "didn't know any theology, perhaps he just about knew the commandments." But he recognized Jesus as the Son of God and "he fell down and worshiped the Lord."

So here we have two contrasting attitudes: on the one hand "those who have doctrine and know things" and on the other "those who have faith." With one certainty: "Faith always leads to witness. Faith is a meeting with Jesus Christ, with God." That meeting "leads to bearing witness," as the apostle James stresses in his letter. He says that "faith without works, faith that doesn't involve you, doesn't lead you to bear witness isn't faith. It's just words. Nothing but words."

Finally, the pope asked us to look to those three figures and ask "for the grace to have faith that bears fruit and leads to proclamation and witness."

Coming Home

Monday, February 24, 2014
Mark 9:14-29

By his tender gestures Jesus never leaves us on our own and always brings us home, calling upon us to become members of his people, his family: the church. This is what Pope Francis said at the Mass celebrated on Monday morning, February 24, in the chapel of St. Martha's Guest House.

For his meditation the pope took his cue from the gospel passage taken from Mark 9:14-29, which tells of the healing of a boy possessed by a demon. The pope set this episode in its context.

"Jesus," he recalled, "was coming down from the mountain where he had been transfigured, and finds these troubled people in disarray. They are disputing and shouting." So "Jesus asks what is happening and the uproar dies down." He begins a conversation with the possessed boy's father, while "everyone listens in silence." When Jesus freed him, "the boy was like a corpse," the gospel tells us, so many thought he was dead. But "Jesus took him by the hand and pulled him up and he was able to stand." The boy was healed and could go home with his family.

So, noted the Holy Father, "all that uproar, that argument, ends in a gesture: Jesus bends down and takes the boy by the hand." And "these gestures by Jesus make us think." Indeed, "when Jesus heals anyone, goes among the people and heals someone, he never leaves that person alone." Because "he isn't a magician, a sorcerer, a witch doctor who goes and heals someone" and then continues on his way. Jesus "makes everyone go home; he doesn't leave them out in the street."

Pope Francis recalled some of the "Lord's beautiful gestures" described in the gospel. "We think," he said, "of that little girl, Jairus' daughter. When Jesus brings her back to life, he looks at her parents and says: give her something to eat!" By that he reassures her father, as if to say: "Your daughter is home, back with her family." Jesus also does the same with "Lazarus when he comes out of the tomb"; he invites the people present to release him from his bandages and help him to walk. The pope also recalled "that dead boy with his widowed mother walking behind his coffin: the Lord raised him and gave him back to his mother."

By all these gestures "Jesus always makes us go home; he never leaves us alone by the wayside." We also find this attitude "in the parables." For example, "the lost coin ends up in the woman's purse with the other coins. And the lost sheep is brought home to the barn with the others."

After all, explained the pope, "Jesus belongs to a people.

Jesus is the promise made to a people." His behavior displays "his identity, which is also membership of that people which had been walking toward the promise since the time of Abraham." So "these gestures of Jesus teach us that every cure, every act of forgiveness always brings us home to our people, which is the church."

To make his idea even clearer, the pope recalled two more examples from the gospel. "So often," he said, "Jesus makes gestures to those who were distanced, condemned by their own fellow citizens, gestures they don't really understand. But they are revolutionary gestures." Among others "think of Zacchaeus, who was actually a crook and a traitor to his country." However, Jesus "has a party in his house." And "think of Matthew, another traitor to his country, who gave money to the Romans." Again, Jesus "has a feast in his house, a great dinner!" The practical teaching is that "when Jesus forgives us, he always makes us go home." Therefore, "Jesus can't be understood apart from the people from whom he comes, God's chosen people, the people of Israel. Or without the people he has called to himself: the church."

Then Pope Francis repeated a thought of Paul VI that he particularly likes: "It's absurd to love Christ without the church; to listen to Christ but not to the church; to follow Christ at the edge of the church." Because "Christ and the church are one. The deepest, greatest theology speaks of a wedding: Christ the bridegroom and the church the bride." So "whenever Christ calls someone, he brings them to the church." We need only think "of the child who comes to be baptized": baptized "into mother church, who stays with her children and at the final moment of their lives entrusts them into the hands of another mother, who is our mother and the mother of Jesus."

"These tender gestures of Jesus," continued the pope, "make us understand that our doctrine—let us call it that—or our following of Christ, isn't just an idea. It's being always at home.

And if one of us strays from home through sin or by mistake, God knows and salvation means going home: with Jesus in the church." So through "tender gestures, one to one, the Lord calls us into his people, his family: our mother, the holy church."

The pope invited those present to think about "those gestures of Jesus: let's imagine how Jesus behaved with so many people" that he met on his way. They are "small gestures" but "gestures of tenderness that tell us about a people, a family, a mother." They remind us "that the salvation he brings us always ends up at home." In conclusion, the pope asked "our mother, the Madonna," for "the grace to understand this mystery."

Partying for War

Tuesday, February 25, 2014
James 4:1-10; Mark 9:3-37

Being appalled by the millions who died in the First World War makes little sense if we aren't also appalled by the numbers who die in the many little wars of today. These wars make countless children die of hunger in refugee camps, while the arms dealers have a ball. At the Mass celebrated on February 25 in the chapel of St. Martha's Guest House, Pope Francis launched an appeal not to remain indifferent in the face of conflicts that continue to make our planet bleed.

He took his cue from the two readings in the day's liturgy, from the Letter of James (4:1-10) and Mark's gospel (9:30-37). The gospel passage makes us think hard. In it we hear that the disciples "were arguing" and "disputing on the way. They were arguing about who was the greatest among them: ambition." As "one or two of them wanted to be the greatest, they had that argument, that quarrel." Thus, said the pope, "their hearts had turned away." The disciples had "estranged hearts" and "when hearts are estranged war arises." That, he stressed, is the essence of "the teaching the apostle James offers us today," directly putting this question in his letter: "Brothers, those conflicts and disputes among you, where do they come from?"

These words "make us reflect" on their aptness today. In fact, noted the pope, "every day in the newspapers we hear about wars." We read: "in such and such a place people were fighting each other" and there were "five dead" and that somewhere else there were other victims and so on. To the point where "we are given a daily tally of the dead." We "get used to reading about these things." For "if we had the patience to list all the wars going on in the world at this moment, we'd certainly fill pages and pages."

Now "it seems that the spirit of war has taken us over." So "there are events to commemorate the centenary of the Great War," in which "so many millions died" and "everyone is appalled." But even today "the same thing is going on but instead of a Great War" there are "small wars all over the place." There are "people divided," who "kill and murder each other to protect their own interests."

"Those conflicts and disputes among you, where do they come from? Do they not come from your cravings that are at war within you?" asks James. Yes, replied the pope, war arises "from within us." Because "wars, hatred, enmity aren't things you go and buy in the market. They are here, in our hearts." He recalled that "when we were children and they told us the story of Cain and Abel, we were all shocked: he killed his brother. Unbelievable!" However, "today millions of brothers are killing one another. But we've gotten used to it!" So "the Great War of 1914 appalls us," whereas "this great war which is all over the place, but sort of hidden, we could say, doesn't appall us." Meanwhile, "so many people die for a strip of land, because of ambition, or hatred, or racial hostility. So many people are dying!"

"Passion," repeated the pope, "leads us to war, to the spirit of the world." So "when there is a conflict we habitually find ourselves in a curious situation" that drives us "to proceed to resolve it by fighting, by the language of war." But what is needed is "the language of peace." And what are the consequences? The pope's answer was succinct: "Think of the starving children in refugee camps: just think of them! That's the result of war!" But his reflection went further. And he added: "And if you like, think of the great halls, the parties given by those who are bosses of the arms industry, the arms manufacturers." So the consequences of war are, on the one hand, "the sick, starving child in a refugee camp," and on the other, "the great parties" and the high life lived by the arms manufacturers.

"But what happens in our hearts?" asked the pope, returning to the Letter of James. "The advice the apostle gives us," he said, "is very simple: Draw near to God, and he will draw near to you." Advice which applies to all of us, because this "spirit of war, which distances us from God, isn't only at work far away from us" but is "also in our homes." As can be seen, for example, in so many "families that are broken because father and mother can't find a way of making peace and prefer war, prefer to quarrel." Truly, "war destroys."

So Pope Francis invited us to "pray for peace," for that "peace which seems to have become a mere word, nothing more." Pray "that this word may have the power to become active." Pray and take heed of the apostle James's exhortation to recognize "your wretchedness." That's where "wars come from: wars in families, wars in neighborhoods, wars everywhere."

St. James's words show us the way to true peace. In the apostle's letter we read: "Cleanse your hands, you sinners, and purify your hearts, you double-minded. Lament and mourn and weep.

Let your laughter be turned into mourning and your joy into dejection." Strong words, which the pope suggested should make us examine our consciences: "Which of us has wept when we read in the newspaper or see on TV the images of so many dead?"

So then, according to Pope Francis, what "a Christian must do today—yes, today, February 25—in the face of so many wars" is, as James says in his letter, humble ourselves "before the Lord"; "lament and mourn and weep." The pope concluded his meditation on peace with a prayer to the Lord to make us "realize this" and save us "from becoming used to all the news of wars."

The Scandal of Inconsistency

Thursday, February 27, 2014
James 5:1-6; Mark 9:41-50

Inconsistent Christians cause scandal because they bear anti-witness to those who don't believe. Jesus uses very strong expressions about consistency, so that hearing them you might say: "But that sounds like a communist!" No: "It's the word of God."

Christian consistency, suggested by the conferring of the sacrament of confirmation, was the theme of Pope Francis' homily at the Mass this morning, Thursday, February 27, in the chapel of St. Martha's Guest House. "Being a Christian," the pope began, "means bearing witness to Jesus Christ." In fact, "a Christian is someone, man or woman, who bears witness to Jesus Christ."

The pope then described the spiritual profile of a Christian, saying that its central element was consistency. In everything in life, he said, we need "to think like a Christian, feel like a Christian, and act like a Christian." That's "Christian consistency," to recognize the Lord's presence "in what we do, feel, and think."

The pope then warned that "if one of these is lacking," then "there's no Christian." For "you can say: I'm a Christian!" But "if you don't live like a Christian, act like a Christian, think like a Christian, and feel like a Christian, something is wrong. There's a certain inconsistency!" All we Christians, said the pope, "are called to bear witness to Jesus Christ." Christians who "usually, commonly live their lives inconsistently do so much harm."

The apostle St. James speaks of them expressly in his letter, read in today's liturgy (5:1-6). He takes issue directly with "certain inconsistent people who boast of being Christians but exploit their laborers." St. James writes: "Listen! The wages of the laborers who mowed your fields, which you kept back by fraud, cry out, and the cries of the harvesters have reached the ears of the Lord of hosts."

"The Lord is powerful," commented the pope, after he had read the text from St. James again. So much so that "if you listen" to these words, "you might think they were spoken by a communist! No, no," declared the pope, "the apostle James said them: they are the word of the Lord!" So the problem is "inconsistency" and "Christians who are inconsistent cause scandal."

Jesus, recalled the pope, referring to today's gospel passage from Mark (9:41-50), speaks out strongly against causing scandal and says: "If any of you scandalize one of these little ones who believes in me—a single one of these brothers or sisters who have faith—it would be better for you if a great millstone were hung around your neck and you were thrown into the sea." Truly, declared the pope, "inconsistent Christians do so much harm," and the strong image used by Jesus is very eloquent. So, he continued, "Christian life must be pursued consistently" but we must also take account "of the temptation to be inconsistent and cause great scandal. That scandal kills people!"

So the consequences are visible to all. Every Christian, commented the pope, has heard people saying, "I believe in God but not in the church, because you Christians say one thing and do another!" These are words that "we've all heard: I believe in God but not in you!" That happens precisely "because of the inconsistency" of Christians, explained the pope.

He went on to say that today's two readings help us "to pray for Christian consistency, to act, feel, and think like Christians." He stressed: "To live a consistently Christian life prayer is necessary, because Christian consistency is a gift of God." It's a gift we must make ourselves ask for, saying: "Lord, make me consistent! Lord, let me never cause scandal! Make me someone who thinks like a Christian, feels like a Christian, and acts like a Christian!" That, said the pope, "is today's prayer for all of us: we need consistency!"

Hence the practical example he gave was significant: "If you find yourself with an atheist who tells you he doesn't believe in God, you can read him a whole library saying that God exists, even prove that God exists, and he still won't have faith." But, continued the pope, "if you show this atheist proof of your consistency, your Christian life, then something will start pressing in his heart." For "it will be the witness you bear which will disturb him and that's what the Holy Spirit will work on."

Pope Francis recalled that "all of us, the whole church," must ask the Lord for "the grace to be consistent." Recognizing that we are sinners, weak, inconsistent, but ever ready to seek forgiveness from God. Indeed, all of us "are able to ask for forgiveness and God never tires of forgiving." So it's important, warned the pope "to have the humility to seek forgiveness" when we haven't been consistent.

Fundamentally, it's a matter of "getting on with life with Christian consistency," bearing witness to our belief in Jesus Christ and knowing that we are sinners. But having "the courage to ask for forgiveness when we go wrong" and "being afraid of causing scandal." The pope's final prayer was: "May the Lord give this grace to all of us."

WHEN LOVE FAILS

Friday, February 28, 2014
MARK 10:1-12

W hen love fails people shouldn't be condemned but sup-
ported. That's what Pope Francis recommended in the
Mass celebrated on Friday, February 28, in the chapel of St. Martha's Guest House. The Genesis story of creation's masterpiece
recognizes love's beauty and grandeur from the start. God makes
Adam and Eve an "image" of the essence of love between a man
and a woman. And also of love between Christ and the church,
the pope explained.

"Jesus was always with people," he said, referring to the day's
gospel passage from Mark (10:1-12). When he was with them
the Lord taught, listened, and healed the sick. But sometimes
among the crowd there were doctors of the law who really wanted
to "test him," hoping in some way to trap him. The reason is
plain, the pope said: "They saw the moral authority Jesus had."
This was self-evident but they felt it to be "a reproach to themselves." So "they tried to trap him to take away that moral authority from him."

Mark's gospel tells how, precisely "in order to test him," the
Pharisees put to Jesus "the problem of divorce." A question
phrased in their usual "style" based on "casuistry." In fact, when
they wanted to make difficulties for Jesus they never asked him
about "an open problem." They preferred to resort to "casuistry,
always putting forth a particular case," and asking him: "Is it lawful or not?"

The "trap" they wanted to set for Jesus is inherent in this way
of seeing things. For, the pope warned, "behind casuistry, behind
casuistic thinking, there's always a trap, always!" A trap "against
people, against us, and against God, always!" So, Mark the evan-
gelist tells us the question the Pharisees put to Jesus is "whether it

is lawful for a man to divorce his wife." Jesus answers it first of all by asking them "what the law says and by explaining why Moses made that law like that."

But the Lord doesn't stop at this first answer and "goes from casuistry to the heart of the problem." So, said the Holy Father, "now he goes back to the days of creation," referring to "such a beautiful" passage from the book of Genesis: "But from the beginning of creation God made them male and female. For this reason a man shall leave his mother and father and be joined to his wife, and the two shall become one flesh. So they are no longer two but one flesh."

Pope Francis reread that passage, explaining that "the Lord is referring to the masterpiece of creation." In fact, God "created light and saw that it was good." Then "he created animals, trees, stars: all were good." But "when he created man" he said "it was very good." For "the creation of man and woman is creation's masterpiece." It was also because "God didn't want man to be alone; he wanted him to have a companion, his companion on the journey."

That, said the pope, was the moment "when love began." The meeting of Adam and Eve is indeed "very poetic." God tells them to carry on together "as one flesh." So that's how "the Lord always takes a casuistic question and brings it back to the beginning of revelation." But, said the pope, "the Lord's masterpiece didn't finish there, in the days of creation." Indeed, the Lord chose "that metaphor to explain the love he had for his people." A great love, "to the point where when the people are unfaithful" he still "speaks words of love to them." Think, he added, "of the Lord's description of his people's unfaithfulness in the sixteenth chapter of the prophet Ezekiel."

Thus "the Lord takes that love from creation's masterpiece to explain the love he has for his people. And this goes a step further: when Paul needs to explain the mystery of Christ, he does so also by referring to his bride. For Christ is married, married to the church, his people." And "just as the Father had married the people of Israel, Christ married his own people."

That, said the pope, "is the story of love. It's the story of creation's masterpiece. Looking at that love, that metaphor, casuistry collapses and becomes sorrow." Sorrow at love's failure: "When leaving father and mother to join with a woman, to become one flesh and live life together, when that love fails—for it so often fails—we should feel sorrow for the failure." At the same time we should also "support those who have suffered that failure in their love." There's no need "to condemn"; we should "stay with them." Above all, we shouldn't "turn their situation into casuistry."

All this, continued the pope, makes us think of a "love plan" for the "path of love in Christian marriage, which God blessed in his creation masterpiece, with a blessing that has never been taken away. Not even original sin destroyed it." And "when we think about this," said the pope, it's natural to recognize "how beautiful love is, how beautiful marriage is, how beautiful the family, all of it." But also "how much love and kindness we should have for brothers and sisters who have suffered from a failure of love in their lives." Love, he recalled, that "begins poetically, because the second creation story of man in the book of Genesis is poetic." And "it finishes poetically in the Bible in Paul's letters when he speaks of the love Christ has for his bride, the church."

But, the pope warned, "here too we must be careful not to let love fail," and end up "speaking of Christ as if he were a 'bachelor.' Christ isn't: he's married to the church! And Christ can't be understood without the church," just as "the church can't be understood without Christ." That, he repeated, "is the great mystery of creation's masterpiece." Pope Francis concluded his meditation by asking the Lord for the grace to understand this mystery "and also for the grace never to fall into the casuistic ways of the Pharisees and doctors of the law."

Nuns and Priests Free from Idolatry

Monday, March 3, 2014
1 Peter 1:3-9; Mark 10:17-27

Ask the Lord to send his church nuns and priests free from "the idolatry of vanity, the idolatry of pride, the idolatry of power, the idolatry of money." Pray knowing that there are vocations, but that we need brave young people, able to respond to the call to follow Jesus "closely" with hearts only for him. That was Pope Francis' "prayer for vocations" during the Mass celebrated on Monday morning, March 3, at St. Martha's.

The pope took his cue from the gospel passage which tells the story of the meeting between Jesus and the rich young man (Mark 10:17-27). "It's a story we've heard so many times," he said. A man "seeks Jesus and kneels down before him." He does so "in front of the whole crowd," because "he was so eager to hear Jesus' words" and "something was urging him in his heart." So "kneeling before Jesus," he asks him what must he do to inherit eternal life. "It was the Holy Spirit moving that's man's heart", noted the pope. Really, he was "a good man, because he had kept the commandments since his youth." But being "good wasn't enough for him: he wanted more! The Holy Spirit was urging him!"

Indeed, the pope continued, "Jesus looked at him and he was happy to hear this." So much so that "the gospel tells us that Jesus loved him." Jesus himself felt the rich young man's enthusiasm. And Jesus makes him a suggestion: "go and sell all you have and come with me to preach the gospel!" But the gospel story tells us, "when he heard these words, the man's face fell and he went sadly away."

That man "had come with hope, with joy to find Jesus. He asked his question. He heard Jesus' words. And he made a decision: to go away." So "that joy urging him on, the joy of the Holy

Spirit, turns to sadness." Indeed, Mark tells us that "he went sadly away because he had great possessions."

The problem, commented the pope, was that "his troubled heart," troubled by "the Holy Spirit, who was pressing him to draw close to Jesus and follow him, was a heart that was chock full." But "he didn't have the courage to empty it. And he made a choice: he chose money!" He had "a heart clogged with money." However, "he wasn't a thief or a criminal. He was a good man: he had never robbed or cheated anyone." His money was "honest money." But "his heart was in thrall to it: it was tied to his money and not free to make a choice." So in the end "his money chose for him."

Mark's gospel continues with Jesus' speech about wealth. But the pope focused in particular on vocations. He turned his mind to all those young people who "feel in their heart that call to come close to Jesus. They are enthusiastic, they aren't afraid to come to Jesus, they aren't ashamed to kneel down before him." Just like the rich young man, with a "public sign," giving "a public demonstration of their faith in Jesus Christ."

For Pope Francis, today too there are so many of these young people who want to follow Jesus. But "when their hearts are full of other things, and they aren't brave enough to empty it, they turn back." Then "their joy becomes sadness." So many young people have that joy which Peter speaks of in his first letter (1:3-9), read in today's liturgy: "So you are filled with an indescribable and glorious joy as you reach the goal of your faith." Indeed, "there are so many" of these young people, "but there's something that stops them."

Really, remarked the pope, "when we ask the Lord" to send "vocations to proclaim the gospel, he does send them." Some people say gloomily: "Father, the world is going so badly: there are no vocations to become nuns or priests, we're going to rack and ruin!" But, the pope stressed, "there are plenty" of vocations. But then, he asked, "if there are plenty, why should we ask the Lord to send them?" The pope's answer was clear: "We must pray that these young people may empty their hearts: empty them of other interests, other loves. So that their hearts become free." That's the true "prayer for vocations: Lord, send nuns, send priests; defend them from the idolatry of vanity, the idolatry of pride, the idolatry of power, the idolatry of money." So "our prayer is to move those hearts to be able to follow Jesus closely."

Returning to the gospel passage, the Holy Father didn't hide the fact that the figure of the rich young man arouses our sympathy, leading us to say: "Poor young man, he was so good and then so unhappy. He didn't go away happy" after his conversation with Jesus. The first thing to do is to pray: "Lord, help these young people to become free and not slaves," so that "their hearts are only for you." In that way, "the Lord's call can get through, can bear fruit."

Pope Francis concluded his meditation by inviting us to recite often "that prayer for vocations." Pray with the awareness "that there are vocations." It's up to us to pray that "they grow strong, that the Lord may be able to enter those hearts and give them that 'indescribable and glorious joy' everyone feels who closely follows Jesus."

Martyrdom Isn't Just a Thing of the Past

Tuesday, March 4, 2014
Mark 10:28-31

Persecution of Christians isn't just something that happened in the past, at the dawn of Christianity. It's a sad reality in our own days. Indeed, "there are more martyrs today than in the early history of the church." Pope Francis was convinced of that and he stressed it this morning, Tuesday, March 4, during the Mass celebrated at St. Martha's. He asked us to reflect on the witness of those brothers and sisters in faith and reminded us that Jesus warned us about this: following him means enjoying his generosity but also "suffering persecutions in his name," as Mark writes in the gospel passage in today's liturgy (10:28-31).

"Jesus," the pope began, "had just been speaking about the danger of riches, about how difficult it is for a rich man to enter the kingdom of heaven. Then Peter asks him a question: 'We have left everything and followed you. What will be our reward?' Jesus is generous and begins by telling Peter: 'Truly I tell you, there is no one who has left house or brothers or sisters or mother or father or children or fields for my sake and for the sake of the gospel, who will not receive a hundredfold now in this age— houses, brothers and sisters, mothers and children, and fields . . .'"

Perhaps, the pope continued, Peter thought: "We're onto a good thing, following Jesus will make us gain so much, a hundredfold." But Jesus "adds two little words: 'with persecutions.' Then he will have eternal life." Basically, he means, "Yes, you've left everything and you'll receive so many things on Earth, but with persecutions." The Holy Father commented it's like "a salad with the dressing of persecution. That's the Christian's reward and that's the way for anyone who wants to follow Jesus. Because it's the way he went himself: he was persecuted."

It's the way of humility, the same way—recalled the bishop of Rome—that Paul speaks of to the Philippians when he says that Jesus became human and "humbled himself to the point of death, even death on a cross." "That's precisely the tenor of Christian life," which is also joy. Indeed, "following Jesus is a joy. In the Beatitudes Jesus says: "Blessed are you when people revile you and persecute you for my sake."

So, said the pope, persecution is one of the Beatitudes. Hence, "as soon as the Holy Spirit came upon them, the disciples began to preach and began to be persecuted. Peter went to prison, Stephen bore witness by his death, just as Jesus had, with false witnesses. Then there have been so many other witnesses right up until today. The cross is always there on the Christian way."

Of course, continued Pope Francis, we can have so many monks and nuns, "so many mothers and fathers, so many brothers and sisters in the church, in the Christian community."

That, he said, "is lovely. But we will also have persecution, because the world won't tolerate Christ's divinity; it won't tolerate the proclamation of the gospel, it won't tolerate the Beatitudes." That's what gives rise to persecution, which may also take the form of words, slander. That's what happened to Christians in the early days, when they suffered calumnies and prison.

"But," said the Holy Father, "we easily forget. Think of all the Christians of sixty years ago, who were locked away in camps, in Nazi and communist prisons: so many, only for being Christians." And that's what happens "today as well," he lamented, despite our conviction that we've become more civilized and have a more highly developed culture.

"I tell you," declared the pope, "that today there are more martyrs than in the church's early days. So many of our brothers and sisters bear witness to Jesus and are persecuted. They are condemned because they possess a bible. They're forbidden to wear a cross." That's "the way of Jesus. But it's a joyful way because the Lord never tries us beyond what we are able to bear."

Certainly, "Christian life isn't a profitable commercial venture," said the pope. It simply means "following Jesus. When we follow Jesus this happens. Let's think whether we have the will to be brave in our witness to Jesus." And he added, "let's also think—it will do us good—of all those brothers and sisters who are unable today to have a book of the gospel or a bible because they're persecuted. Let's think about those brothers and sisters who can't go to Mass because it's forbidden. How often a priest meets them in secret and they pretend they're at table having tea and celebrate the Mass in secret. That happens today." Hence his concluding invitation: "Let's think: am I prepared to carry the cross like Jesus? To bear persecutions in order to witness to Jesus like those brothers and sisters who are being persecuted today? That thought will do us all good."

The Christian Way

Thursday, March 6, 2014
Luke 9:22-25

Pope Francis' Lenten invitation was to rediscover the fruitfulness of a life lived in a Christian way. He spoke about it this morning, Thursday, March 6, during the Mass celebrated at St. Martha's. Commenting on the gospel passage from Luke (9:22-25) in the day's liturgy, the pope presented it as a reflection following the story of the rich young man who wanted to follow Jesus "but then went sadly away, because he had so much money and was too attached to it to give it up." Then Jesus spoke about "the risk of having so much money," ending up with the clear message: "You cannot serve two masters, God and money."

At the beginning of Lent the church "makes us read, makes us listen to that message," noted the pope. A message, he said, which "we could call the Christian way: 'If any want to become my followers, let them deny themselves and take up their cross daily and follow me.' For Jesus himself was the first to go along that road." The bishop of Rome repeated the words from Luke's gospel: "The son of man must undergo great suffering, and be rejected by the elders, chief priests, and scribes, and be killed, and rise again on the third day. "So," he stressed, "we can't think of Christian life

apart from that way, that road which he was the first to go along."
It's "the way of humility, humiliation, self-emptying" so that "the
Christian way without the cross actually isn't Christian." Also "if
the cross is a cross without Jesus, it isn't Christian."

Adopting a Christian way of life means "taking up the cross
with Jesus and carrying on." Christ himself showed us that way
by emptying himself. Although he was equal to God, noted the
pope, he didn't boast about it and he didn't "regard it as something to be exploited, but emptied himself" and became "a slave
for all of us."

That way of life "will save us, will bring us joy and make us
fruitful. For that way by which we deny ourselves is one that
brings life; it's the opposite of the way of selfishness, the way
leading us to become attached to all kinds of goods for their own
sake." The Christian way is "open to others, because it's the way
of Jesus." So it's a way of "self-emptying in order to give life. The
Christian way is the way of humility, gentleness, kindness. Anyone who wants to save their life will lose it. Jesus repeats that in
the gospel. Remember when he speaks of the grain of wheat: if
the seed doesn't die it can't bear fruit" (cf. John 12:24).

It's a road to be followed "with joy, because," explained the
pope, "it's Jesus himself who brings us joy. Following Jesus is a
joy." But, he repeated, we must follow him in his way "and not
in the way of the world." Each of us must do what we can: the
important thing is to do it "to give life to others, not life for ourselves. It's the spirit of generosity."

So that's the way to go: "Humility, service, not selfishness, not
feeling ourselves to be important or acting arrogantly toward others: I'm a Christian . . .!" Here Pope Francis quoted *The Imitation of Christ*, which, he said, gives us some very fine advice: *ama
nesciri et pro nihilo reputari*, 'love to be unknown and counted as
nothing.' That's Christian humility. Jesus was the first to practice
it."

"Think of Jesus who goes ahead of us," he continued, "who guides us along the way. That's our joy and that's our fruitfulness: walking with Jesus. Other joys aren't fruitful; as the Lord says, they think only of gaining the whole world but end up losing it and ruining themselves."

So "at the beginning of Lent," the pope concluded, "let us ask the Lord to teach us that Christian way of service, joy, self-emptying and fruitfulness with him, as he desires."

THE SPIRIT OF HYPOCRISY

Friday, March 7, 2014
ISAIAH 58:1-9A; MATTHEW 9:14-15

The "spirit of hypocrisy" makes us forget how to cherish a sick person, a child, an old person. And it keeps us from looking into the eyes of someone when we give them alms and withdraw our hand at once so that it won't get dirty. Pope Francis gave us a lesson in never "being ashamed of our brother's flesh" during the Mass celebrated on the morning of March 7 in the chapel of St. Martha's Guest House.

On the Friday after Ash Wednesday, explained the pope, the church offers us a meditation on the real meaning of fasting. And it does so by means of two incisive readings, taken from the prophet Isaiah (58:1-9a) and Matthew's gospel (9:14-15). "Today's readings," the pope began, "speak of the spirit of hypocrisy, of formalism in fulfilling his commandments, in this case fasting." For "Jesus returns so often to the subject of hypocrisy when he sees the doctors of the church thinking they're perfect: they fulfill everything in the commandments as if it were a formality."

Here, said the pope, we find "a problem of memory," which

is "a two-faced way of carrying on." Actually, hypocrites "have forgotten that they were chosen by God as members of a people, not for themselves alone. They've forgotten the history of their people, that history of salvation, election, covenant, promise," which comes straight from the Lord. By doing so, "they have reduced that history to a matter of ethics. Religious life for them was a matter of ethics."

That "explains why in Jesus' time, theologians tell us, there were about three hundred commandments" which had to be kept. But "receiving a father's love from the Lord, becoming as a people, and then turning it into an ethical system" means "rejecting that gift of love." After all, he said, hypocrites "are good folk; they do everything that should be done, they seem good." But "they're ethicists, ethicists without kindness, because they have lost the sense of belonging to a people."

"God gives salvation to a people, by belonging to a people," explained the pope. So "we can understand how the prophet Isaiah speaks to us today about fasting, penance. What is the fasting the Lord wants? Fasting that is related to a people, the people to whom we belong: our people, among whom we are called, among whom we live."

Pope Francis reread the passage from the book of Isaiah: "Is not this the fast that I choose: to loose the bonds of injustice, to undo the thongs of the yoke, to let the oppressed go free, and to break every yoke? Is it not to share your bread with the hungry, and bring the homeless poor into your house; when you see the naked to cover them, and not hide yourself from your own kin?"

Here, the bishop of Rome repeated, is the true meaning of "fasting. To care for your brother's life, not to be ashamed of your brother's flesh, as Isaiah himself says." In fact, "our perfection, our holiness progresses with our people, among whom we are chosen and to whom we belong." And "our greatest act of holiness lies in the body of our brother, and the body of Jesus Christ."

Thus, he stressed, "our act of holiness today—of us who are here before the altar—isn't hypocritical fasting. It's not being ashamed of the body of Christ, which comes to us here today: it's the mystery of the body and blood of Christ. It means sharing our bread with the hungry, healing the sick, the old, those who can't give us anything in return: that's what not being ashamed of the body means."

"God's salvation," the pope repeated, "is for a people. A people that progresses, a people consisting of brothers and sisters who are not ashamed of one another." But precisely that, he insisted, "is the most difficult kind of fasting: the fasting of kindness. Kindness brings us to that." For "perhaps," he explained, quoting the gospel, "the priest who passed by on the other side of that wounded man thought,"—referring to the commandments of the time—"if I touch his blood, that wounded flesh, I'll become unclean and I won't be able to keep the Sabbath! He was ashamed of the body of that man. That's hypocrisy!" On the other hand, noted the Holy Father, "when the sinner was passing and saw the wounded man, he saw his brother's body, the body of a man belonging to his people, a Son of God like himself. And he wasn't ashamed."

"So today the church suggests" a true and thorough examination of conscience by a series of questions the pope put to those present: "Am I ashamed of my brother or my sister's body? When I give alms, do I drop the money without touching the person's hand? And if I should touch it, do I do this at once?" he asked with a gesture of withdrawing his hand sharply. Again: "When I give alms, do I look my brother or sister in the eyes? When I know that someone is sick, do I go to them? Do I greet them warmly?"

To complete this examination of conscience, said the pope, "there's a sign that may perhaps help us." It's a question of "do I know how to touch sick people, old people, children tenderly? Or have I lost the sense of tenderness?" Hypocrites, he continued, no longer know how to touch others with tenderness, they've forgotten how to do it. So that's the advice: "not to be ashamed of our brother's flesh: it's our flesh." For, concluded the pope, "we will be judged" by our behavior toward "that brother, that sister" and certainly not by "hypocritical fasting."

No One Can Judge You

Monday, March 17, 2014
Daniel 9:4-10; Luke 6:36-38

Who am I to judge other people? That's the question to ask ourselves to make room for mercy, the right attitude for building peace among people, nations, and ourselves. In order to be merciful women and men we need first of all to recognize that we are sinners and then open our hearts to forget the wrongs that have been done to us.

Pope Francis focused his homily on mercy in the Mass celebrated on Monday morning, March 17, in the chapel of St. Martha's Guest House. Referring to the passages from the book of the prophet Daniel (9:4-10) and Luke's gospel (6:36-38), the Holy Father explained that "Jesus' invitation to mercy was to draw nearer to God our Father and become more like him: be merciful as your Father is merciful." But, the pope recognized immediately, "it's not easy to understand that attitude of mercy, because we're accustomed to presenting others with a bill: you've done that, so now you have to do this in return." In short, "we judge, that's our attitude and we don't" leave "any bit of room for understanding and mercy."

"In order to be merciful two attitudes are needed," said the pope. First, "self-knowledge." In the first reading Daniel makes his prayer on behalf of the people, confessing they're sinners in God's sight and says: "We have done this but you are just. Justice is on your side, O Lord, but open shame falls on us." Thus, said the pope, commenting on the passage, "God's justice toward his repentant people becomes mercy and forgiveness." He invited us also to "make a little room for that attitude." The first step toward "becoming merciful is to recognize that we've done so many wrong things: we are sinners!" We need to be able to say: "Lord, I'm ashamed of these things I've done in my life." For "even if none of us has murdered anyone," we've still committed "so many daily sins. Recognizing that we have done something against the Lord and being ashamed before God is a grace: the grace of being sinners!" It's simple—but at the same time "so hard"—to say: "I'm a sinner and I'm ashamed in your sight and I ask you for forgiveness."

"Our father Adam," said the pope, "gave us an example of what we shouldn't do." For he blames the woman for eating the fruit and justifies himself saying: "I haven't sinned," it's she "who made me do it!" But then Eve does the same and blames the serpent. In fact, repeated the Holy Father, it's important to recognize that we've sinned and need God's forgiveness. We mustn't seek excuses and "put the blame on others." Perhaps, "someone else helped me" to sin, "led the way: but I did it!" And "if we do this, so many good things will follow: we'll be proper human beings." What's more, "with this attitude of repentance we become able to be merciful, because we feel God's mercy upon us." So in the Lord's Prayer we not only pray "forgive us our trespasses," but also "as we forgive them who trespass against us." For indeed "if I don't forgive, I'm not playing the game right, I'm 'offside.'"

The second attitude needed in order to be merciful "is to expand our hearts." Actually, "shame and repentance expand a heart that is narrow and selfish, because they make room for a merciful God to forgive us." But what does expanding our hearts mean? First and foremost, when we recognize we are sinners we mustn't look to what other people have done. The basic question to ask becomes: "Who am I to judge? Who am I to gossip about that? Who am I, who have done the same or worse?" After all, "the Lord says in the gospel: do not judge, and you will not be judged; do not condemn and you will not be condemned; forgive and you will be forgiven. Give, and it will be given to you: a good measure, pressed down, shaken together, running over, will be put into your lap." That's "the generosity of heart," which the Lord describes, using "the image of people who went to get grain and spread out their aprons in order to get more!" And "a great heart doesn't interfere in other people's lives, doesn't condemn, but forgives and forgets," just as "God has forgotten and forgiven my own sins."

So in order to be merciful it's necessary to call upon the Lord—"because it's a grace"—and to "have these two attitudes: recognizing our own sins and being ashamed" and forgetting the sins and wrongs done by others. That's how "the merciful man and woman have great hearts: they always excuse others and think of their own sins." If someone says to them: "Did you see what so and so has done?" they have the kindness to reply, "But I've done quite a lot of things myself."

That, suggested the pope, is "the way of mercy we must ask for." If "all of us, countries, people, families, neighborhoods had that attitude," he exclaimed, "what great peace there would be in the world, and in our hearts, because mercy brings us peace!" He concluded: "Always remember: who am I to judge? Be ashamed and expand your heart; may the Lord give us this grace!"

Don't Be Cosmetic Christians

Tuesday, March 18, 2014
Isaiah 1:10, 16-20; Matthew 23:1-12

Christians who think they can save themselves on their own "are hypocrites"; they are "cosmetic Christians." Lent is the right time to change our lives and draw near to Jesus, asking for forgiveness. It's the time to repent and be ready to bear witness to his light by taking care of those in need. Pope Francis offered us another Lenten reflection this morning, Tuesday, March 18, at the Mass celebrated in St. Martha's.

He introduced his homily by saying: "Lent is a time to draw closer to the Lord." After all, he explained, the word itself says as much for "Lent" means conversion. Today's first reading, he noted, referring to the passage from Isaiah (1:10, 16-20), "begins with a call to repent. The Lord calls us to conversion; and he calls two sinful cities," Sodom and Gomorrah. He invites them: "Repent, change your life, draw near to the Lord." This, he explained, "is the invitation Lent offers us: forty days to draw near to the Lord, to come closer to him. We all need to change our lives." There's no point in saying: "But Father, I'm not such a big sinner . . ." because "we all have something and if we look into our souls, we'll find something that isn't right, every one of us."

So Lent "invites us to change, to set our lives in order," said the pope. That's what enables us to draw closer to the Lord. He's ready to forgive us.

The pope then referred back to the words of the first reading: "Though your sins are like scarlet, they shall be like snow." He continued: "'I change your soul': that's what Jesus tells us. And what does he ask of us? To draw near. To draw near to him. Draw near to the Father who is waiting to forgive us. And Jesus gives us advice: 'Don't be like the hypocrites.'" To explain this Pope Francis then referred to the gospel passage from Matthew

(23:1-12), which had just been read: "We read in the gospel: that's not the way the Lord wants us to approach him. He wants us to approach him sincerely, truly. What do the hypocrites do? They disguise themselves. They make themselves out to be good. They put on holy picture faces, they pray lifting up their eyes to heaven, letting themselves be seen; they feel they're better than other people, they despise others." And they boast of being good Catholics because they're on good terms with benefactors, bishops, and cardinals.

"That's hypocrisy," stressed the pope. "And the Lord says no," because no one should feel they're good simply in their own estimation. "We all need to be justified," repeated the bishop of Rome, "and the only one who justifies us is Jesus Christ. So that's why we need to draw near to him and not be just cosmetic Christians." When appearances fade, "the reality is revealed and these are not Christians. What's the touchstone? The Lord himself tells us in the first reading: 'Wash yourselves; make yourselves clean; remove the evil of your doings from before my eyes; cease to do evil, learn to do good.'" That, he repeated, is the call.

But "what is the sign that we are on the right road? Scripture always tells us: defend the oppressed; take care of your neighbor, the sick, the poor, the needy, the ignorant. That's the touchstone." And again: "Hypocrites can't do this, because they're so full of themselves that they're blind to others." But "when we carry on a bit further and draw nearer to the Lord, the Father's light makes us see these things and we go and help our fellow human beings. That's the sign of conversion."

Of course, he added, that's "not the whole story of conversion; because conversion is an encounter with Jesus Christ. But the sign that we are with Jesus is this: looking after our fellow human beings, the poorest, the sick, as the Lord teaches us in the gospel."

So Lent is to "change our lives, alter our lives, to draw closer to the Lord." Hypocrisy is "the sign that we are far from the Lord."

The hypocrite "saves himself, or at least thinks he does," continued the Holy Father, whereas the sign that we have drawn closer to the Lord in a spirit of repentance and forgiveness "is that we take care of our brothers and sisters in need." Hence the conclusion: "May the Lord give all of us light and courage: light to know what is going on within us and courage to be converted, to draw closer to the Lord. It's beautiful to be close to the Lord."

THE ONE WITH NO NAME

Thursday, March 20, 2014
JEREMIAH 17:5-10; LUKE 16:19-31

There's a "more than magic" word which can open "the door of hope we can't even see" and give back our name if we've lost it because we trusted only in ourselves and human power. That word is "Father" and it is said with the certainty of hearing God's voice answering us and calling us "my child." Pope Francis offered this Lenten meditation on the heart of the faith at the Mass celebrated on Thursday, March 20, in the chapel of St. Martha's House.

The invitation to "trust in the Lord always" comes from today's liturgy, said the pope in his homily. In fact "today's first reading (Jeremiah 17:5-10) begins with a curse: 'Cursed are those who trust in human beings.'" And "the same curse comes in other biblical passages, perhaps in different words." For example: "Cursed are they who trust in themselves." It's always "cursed are those" who trust only in their own strength, "because they bear a curse within them."

On the other hand, the pope continued, "the opposite" is "blessed are those who trust in the Lord," because, as we read in the Bible, they are like "a tree planted by water, sending out its roots toward the stream. It shall not fear when heat comes, and its leaves shall stay green; in the year of drought it is not anxious, and it doesn't cease to bear fruit."

"That image," he explained, "makes us think of Jesus' words about a house: happy is the man who builds his house on rock, on something solid. On the other hand, unhappy is the one who builds on sand: he's insecure." So "God's word today teaches us that our secure trust is only in the Lord: it doesn't work with anyone else; others don't save us, they don't give us life, they don't give us joy." But "they bring us death, drought."

It's a clear teaching with which we all agree, said the pope. "But our problem is that our hearts are untrustworthy," as scripture tells us. So even though we know we are mistaken, we still "like to trust in ourselves or in some friend or in some good situation or some ideology," indulging "that tendency" to decide for ourselves where to place "our trust." With the result that "the Lord gets rather left out."

But, the pope asked, "why are they who trust in themselves cursed? Because," he replied, "that trust makes them look to themselves alone; it encloses them within themselves, with no horizons, no open doors, no windows." So they end up becoming "people shut off within themselves" and "who won't have salvation," because "they can't save themselves."

The pope then referred to the gospel passage from Luke (16:19-31), which tells the story of "a rich man who had everything, who dressed in purple and who feasted sumptuously every day and lived in luxury." And "he was so content that he didn't notice that at his gate lay a poor man named Lazarus, full of sores, a tramp, and like any good tramp, with dogs." Lazarus "lay there, starving, eating only what fell from the rich man's table: the scraps." And, the pope added, "perhaps when Jesus told this story, he remembered the Canaanite woman, who had asked him to heal her daughter: she only asked for the scraps" which are given to the dogs.

The gospel passage suggests a reflection, said the Holy Father: "We know the name of the tramp: he was called Lazarus. But what was the rich man's name? He hasn't got one!" Indeed, "that's the strongest curse" for someone who "trusts in himself or in human strength or powers and not in God: losing his name!" To the point where when he's asked "what's your name?" he replies not with his own name but "account number such and such of such and such a bank," or by listing "all his properties, his villas" and "things, idols."

Now, "when we look at the two people" in the gospel story— "the poor man who has a name and trusts in the Lord and the rich man who has lost his name and trusts in himself"—we "say: it's true, we must trust in the Lord!" However, "all of us have that weakness, that frailty of putting our hopes in ourselves or our friends or only in human powers. And we forget the Lord." That attitude takes us far from the Lord, "along the road of unhappiness," just like the rich man in the gospel, who "ends up unhappy because he has condemned himself." So that's the real meaning of the biblical expression: "Blessed are those who trust in the Lord; cursed are those who trust in themselves or human powers."

This meditation is particularly suited to Lent, said the pope. So "today it will do us good to ask ourselves: where do I put my trust?" In the Lord? Or am I a pagan who trusts in things, in idols I have made myself? Have I still got a name or have I begun to lose my name and just call myself 'I'?" with all its conjugations: "me, with me, for me, only me: always selfish, me!" That, he stressed, is a way of living that certainly "doesn't bring us salvation."

Still referring to the gospel, Pope Francis pointed out that in spite of everything, "there's a door of hope open to all those who have put their trust in human beings or in themselves, who have lost their names." Because "in the end, there's always a possibility." The rich man shows this "when he realizes he has lost his name, lost everything; he lifts up his eyes and says just one word: 'Father!' And God's reply is also just one word: 'Son!'" That goes for all those who during their lives have "put their trust in human beings, in themselves, ending up losing their names, losing their dignity: it's still possible to utter that word that is more than magic, greater, more powerful than magic: 'Father!'" For we know that "he's always waiting to open a door for us, which we can't see. And he will say to us: 'My child!'"

In conclusion the pope asked "the Lord for the grace to give us all the wisdom to trust only in him and not in things, not in human strength: only in him." And to anyone who loses that trust, may God at least "give light" to recognize and utter "that saving word, which opens a door and enables us to hear the Father's voice saying: my child."

THE IMPRISONED WORD

Friday, March 21, 2014
GENESIS 37:3-4, 12-13, 17-28; MATTHEW 21:33-43, 45

Humility and prayer, in the church, are the antidote to the doctoring of God's word and the temptation to take control of it, interpreting it as we please and caging the Holy Spirit. That was the gist of the pope's meditation at the Mass celebrated on Friday morning, March 21, in the chapel of St. Martha's Guest House.

"During these days of Lent the Lord comes close to us, and the church leads us on toward the Easter Triduum, toward Jesus' death and resurrection," said the pope, referring to the two readings in the liturgy. In the first, taken from Genesis (37:3-4,

12-13, 17-28), we hear the story of "Joseph, sold by his brothers for twenty shekels, which is a prophecy and image of Jesus." The second reading, from Matthew's gospel (21:33-43, 45), gives us "that parable which Jesus tells the people and the Pharisees, priests and the elders of the people to make them realize how they've gone wrong." So here, he explained, we have "a drama, not of the people—because the people understood that Jesus was a great prophet—but of some of the people's leaders, elders whose ears were not open to the word of God." In fact, they "listened to Jesus, but instead of seeing God's promise in him, or recognizing him as a great prophet, they were afraid."

Basically, noted the pope, "they felt the same way as Herod." They too said: "This man is a revolutionary, let's put a stop to him in time; we must put a stop to him! That's why they tried to catch him out; they tried to test him so that he fell into a trap and they could get him: it was a persecution against Jesus!" But why that persecution? "Because," answered the pope, "they weren't open to God's word, they were enclosed within their own selfishness."

That was the context in which "Jesus tells this parable: God bequeathed land with a vineyard he himself had planted." We read in the gospel that the householder "planted a vineyard, and set a hedge around it, and dug a winepress in it, and built a tower." These are all the things "he did with so much love." Then "he let the vineyard out to tenants."

That's exactly what "God has done with us: he has leased us our lives" and also given us "the promise" that he would come and save us. "But these tenants," noted Pope Francis, "saw a good business opportunity here, they were onto a good thing: the vineyard is beautiful; let's take it, it's ours!" So "when the time came to gather the fruits, the master's servants arrived to collect the harvest. But the tenants, who had already taken over the vineyard, said no, let's drive them away; it's ours!"

Jesus' parable, explained the pope, is a precise account of "the drama of those people but also our own drama." Actually, those people had "taken control of the word of God. God's word had become their word. A word in accordance with their interests, their ideologies, their theologies, for their own use." To the point where "each of them interprets it as they please, in accordance with their own interests." And "they kill to protect those interests." That's also what happened to Jesus, because "the chief priests and Pharisees realized he was talking about them when they heard the parable" and so "they tried to arrest him and put him to death."

But in that way "God's word becomes dead, becomes imprisoned." And "the Holy Spirit becomes caged within their devices and desires. The same thing happens with us, when we aren't open to the newness of God's word, when we aren't obedient to God's word." But disobeying God's word is like saying that "this word no longer belongs to God: now it's ours!"

As "God's word is dead in the hearts of these people, it can also become dead in our own hearts." And yet, declared the Holy Father, the word "never stops there because it's alive in the hearts of the ordinary people, the humble people, the people of God." In fact, when they tried to arrest Jesus they were afraid of the people, who thought he was a prophet. It was "the crowd of ordinary people who followed Jesus, because what Jesus said did them good and warmed their hearts." Those ordinary people "didn't use God's word for their own ends," but simply "felt and tried to become a little better."

At this point the pope suggested we should think about "what we can do so as not to kill God's word, not take over that word, to be receptive, not to cage the Holy Spirit." He mentioned two things: humility and prayer.

Certainly, he noted, "those people weren't humble who didn't accept God's word but said: yes, that's God's word but I interpret it in accordance with my own interests!" In that way "they were proud, self-sufficient, they were 'doctors' in quotes": people who "thought they had the power to change the meaning of God's word." For "only the humble have open hearts to receive God's word." Nevertheless, we should point out, he said that "there were also good and humble priests, humble Pharisees who welcomed God's word: for example, the gospel tells us about Nicodemus." So "the first thing needed to listen to God's word" is humility, because "without humility you can't receive God's word." The second thing is prayer. For the people in the parable "didn't pray, they had no need to pray: they felt they were secure, they felt strong, they felt they were gods."

So "we must listen to God's word with humility and prayer and obey it in the church." Then "we won't go the way of those people in the parable; we won't kill to defend that word which we believe to be God's word" but which has really become "a word completely altered by us."

In conclusion the pope asked "the Lord for the grace of humility, to look to Jesus as the savior who speaks to us: speak to me! Each of us must say: speak to me!" And "when we read the gospel: speak to me!" Hence the invitation "to open our hearts to the Holy Spirit who gives power to this word" and "pray, pray a lot that we may be able to welcome this word and obey it."

SAVED ON THE MARGINS

Monday, March 24, 2014
II KINGS 5:1-15A; LUKE 4:24-30

God finds us and saves us when we are marginalized, when we are on the edge. Pope Francis reminded us of this at the Mass celebrated on Monday morning, March 24, in the chapel of St. Martha's Guest House, focusing his homily on a pressing call to humility.

To explain what is meant by being saved "on the margins" the pope referred to the day's liturgy, which presented two particularly eloquent passages taken from the second book of Kings (5:1-15a) and Luke's gospel (4:24-30). In the gospel passage, noted the Holy Father, Jesus says he can do no miracles in his Nazareth "for lack of faith": in the place where he had grown up "they didn't have faith." For Jesus said, "No prophet is acceptable in his own country." Then the pope recalled the story of Naaman the Syrian with the prophet Elisha, heard in the first reading, and the story of the widow of Sidon with the prophet Elijah.

"At that time lepers and widows were marginalized," stressed the pope. In particular, "widows lived on public charity; they didn't belong to normal society," and lepers had to live outside the city, far away from people.

So, we read in the gospel, in the synagogue at Nazareth "Jesus tells us that there will be no miracles here: you don't accept the prophet here because you don't need him, you are too safe." The people standing in front of Jesus were "so secure in their 'faith' in quotes, so secure in their observance of the commandments, that they didn't need any other salvation." An attitude, explained the pope, that is "the story of keeping the commandments without faith: I can save myself on my own because I go to the synagogue every Saturday, I try to obey the commandments"; and "that fellow can't come and tell me that this leper and this widow are better than me; they're outcasts!"

But Jesus' words say the opposite. He says: "Look if you don't think of yourself as being the margins, you won't have salvation! That's humility, the way of humility: to feel yourself so marginalized" that you "need the Lord's salvation. He alone saves, not our observance of regulations."

But we are told as we read on in the passage from Luke that

Jesus' teaching was not to the liking of the people of Nazareth; indeed, "they became indignant and wanted to kill him." It was "the same indignation" that also possessed Naaman the Syrian, according to the Old Testament story. In order to be cured of leprosy, explained the bishop of Rome, Naaman "went to the king with many gifts, a lot of money: he felt secure, he was the commander of the army." But the prophet Elisha invited him to become marginalized and go and wash "seven times" in the River Jordan. An invitation, the pope recognized, that must have sounded "a bit ridiculous" to him. So much so that Naaman "felt humiliated; he became indignant and went off," just like "those in the synagogue at Nazareth." The Bible, noted the pope, uses the same word for both situations: they became "indignant."

For Naaman is asked to make "a gesture of humility, to obey like a child: to become ridiculous!" But he reacts with indignation: "We have so many fine rivers of Damascus, like the Abana and the Parpar, and am I to go and wash seven times in that little stream? That's absurd!" However, he has servants with good sense, who "help him to marginalize himself, to make an act of humility." Naaman comes out of the river cured of his leprosy.

So, stressed the pope, "that's today's message in this third week of Lent: if we want to be saved, we must choose the way of humility, humiliation." Consider Mary's witness, who "in her canticle doesn't say she's happy because God has looked upon her virginity, her goodness, her sweetness, all the virtues she had," but she rejoices "because the Lord has looked upon the humility of his servant, has looked upon her littleness." That's "the humility that looks to the Lord."

We too, declared the pope, "must learn the wisdom of becoming marginalized so that the Lord may find us." Indeed, "God won't find us in the midst of all our securities. No, the Lord doesn't go there! He will find us if we are marginalized, in our sins, our mistakes, our need for spiritual healing, for salvation. That's where the Lord will find us."

That, he reiterated, "is the way of humility. Christian humility isn't a virtue" which makes us say: "I'm good for nothing." No, "Christian humility is telling the truth: I'm a sinner!" Basically, it's simply a matter of "telling the truth, and that's the truth about ourselves." But, the pope concluded, there is also "another truth: God saves us! But he saves us when we are marginalized. He doesn't save us in our security." Hence his prayer to God to give us "the grace to have the wisdom to become marginalized; the grace of humility to receive the Lord's salvation."

Salvation Is a Gift

Tuesday, March 25, 2014
Luke 1:26-38; Hebrews 10:4-10

Salvation "can't be bought or sold" because "it's a completely free gift." But in order to receive it God asks us to have "a humble, receptive, and obedient heart." Pope Francis said this during the Mass celebrated on Tuesday morning, March 25, in the chapel of St. Martha's Guest House. He invited us to "celebrate and give thanks to God," because "today we commemorate a definitive stage along the way" to salvation, a journey which human beings "began on the day they left paradise."

"Today we celebrate the feast of that journey from one mother to another mother, from one father to another father," explained the pope. He invited us to contemplate "the image of Eve and Adam, and the image of Mary and Jesus" to see the course of history with God, who always walks together with his people. So, he continued, "today we can embrace the Father, who has become like one of us, thanks to the blood of his Son, and saves us: the Father who awaits us every day." Let us say "thank you, thank you, Lord, because today you tell us you have given us salvation."

In his reflection the pope took his cue from the commandment given to Adam and Eve: the task to till the earth and subdue it and to be fruitful. "It's the promise of redemption," he said. "With this commandment, this promise, they embarked on a journey." A "long journey over many centuries," but it began "with an act of disobedience." Actually, Adam and Eve "were deceived, they were seduced. Satan seduced them saying: you will be like God!" So they were overcome with "arrogance and pride," and "they fell into temptation to take over God's place through pride." And that's exactly "the attitude that Satan has himself."

Adam and Eve "founded a people." And "they didn't make this journey alone: the Lord was with them." He accompanied humanity all along its way, "which began with an act of disobedience and ended with an act of obedience." In order to explain it, Pope Francis recalled, "The Second Vatican Council adopts a beautiful phrase from St. Irenaeus of Lyons, who says: the knot tied by Eve through her disobedience was undone by Mary through her obedience." And, he added, the church also describes this journey in a prayer she recites: "Lord, you who have marvelously created humanity and yet more marvelously restored it . . ." So "it's a journey where God's marvels are multiplied, they increase!"

God always stays "with his people on the journey; he sends the prophets and he sends people who explain the law." But "why," asked the pope, "does the Lord walk so lovingly with his people? To soften our hearts," was the reply. And in fact the Bible explicitly says: I will turn your heart of stone into a heart of flesh.

Basically, the Lord wants "to soften our hearts" so that we can receive "that promise he made in paradise: by one man came sin, by another man will come salvation." It's "that long journey" which helped "all of us to have a more human heart, that was closer to God, less proud, less self-sufficient."

"Today," explained the pope, "the liturgy speaks to us about that journey of restoration. It speaks to us of obedience, of receptivity to God's word." One idea, noted the pope, "is very clear" in the second reading, taken from the letter to the Hebrews (10:4-10): "For it's impossible for the blood of bulls and goats to take away sin."

That means "salvation can't be bought or sold. It's a gift, it's free." Since "we can't save ourselves on our own, salvation is a totally free gift." As we read in Hebrews, it can't be bought with "the blood of bulls and goats." It "can't be bought," but what "salvation demands is a humble heart, a receptive heart, an obedient heart, like Mary's." So "the model for this journey of salvation is God himself, his Son. As Paul says, he emptied himself and became obedient to the point of death, death on a cross."

So what is meant by "a journey of humility, humiliation"? It simply means, Pope Francis concluded, "saying I am a man, I am a woman, a man or a woman under obedience and with a listening heart."

Pontifical Mass for Italian Members of Parliament at the Altar of St. Peter's Chair in the Vatican Basilica

Thursday, March 27, 2014
Jeremiah 7:23-24; Luke 11:11-14

The readings the church offers us today can be described as a conversation between God's reproaches and human self-justification. The Lord God laments. He laments that he has not been listened to throughout history. It's always the same: 'Listen to my voice . . . I will be your God . . . You will be happy . . .' 'But they don't listen, they don't lend an ear to my words. On the contrary: they stubbornly follow their own wicked hearts. Instead of turning to me, they turn their backs on me' (Jeremiah 7:23-24). It's the story of the *unfaithfulness* of the people of God

God laments because it was a very great labor for the Lord to get rid of idolatry from his people's hearts and make them obey his word. They went the right way for a little while and then turned back again. And so on for centuries and centuries until Jesus arrived.

The same thing happened with the Lord, with Jesus. Some people were saying: 'He's the Son of God, he's a great prophet!' but others, whom we hear about in today's gospel, were saying: 'No, he's a sorcerer who heals by the power of Satan.' The people of God were alone, and that ruling class—the doctors of the law, the Sadducees, the Pharisees—had closed minds, and were rigid in their behavior and ideology. It was that class who wouldn't listen to the word of the Lord, and in order to justify themselves they said what we heard in the gospel today. It's the same as saying 'He's a soldier of Beelzebub or Satan or one of Satan's gang'; it's the same thing. They couldn't hear: they were so closed-minded, distant from the people and that's true. Jesus looks at the people and he's moved, because he sees them as 'sheep without a shepherd,' as the gospel says. He goes about among the poor, the sick, everybody, widows, lepers, and heals them. He speaks to them in such a way that they are amazed: 'But this man speaks with authority!' He speaks differently from that ruling class which had become distant from the people. They were only interested in their own things: their group, their party, their internal feuds. Then there were the people . . . They had abandoned the flock. And were they sinners? Yes. Yes, we are all sinners. All of us here are sinners. But they were more than sinners: the hearts of those leaders, that little group, had become so hardened over time, that it was impossible for them to hear the word of the Lord. And from being sinners, they slid into becoming corrupt. And it's so difficult for a corrupt person to turn back. A sinner, yes, because the Lord is merciful and he awaits us all. But the corrupt person is fixated on his own affairs, and those leaders were corrupt. That's why they justified themselves, because Jesus in his simplicity, but also with his power of God, annoyed them. Step by step, they ended up convincing themselves that they should kill Jesus, and one of them said: 'It's better that one man should die for the people.'

They had lost their way. They resisted the Lord's salvation of love, so they slid away from faith, from a theology of faith to a theology of duty: 'You must do this and this and this . . .' Jesus accuses them with that ugly word: 'Hypocrites! You lay heavy burdens on the people's shoulders. And yourselves? You don't lift a finger to help! Hypocrites!' They've rejected the Lord's love, and thus they've rejected the way of freedom offered by the Lord and gone for the logic of necessity, where there's no room for the Lord. In the dialectic of freedom there's the good Lord who loves us, loves us so much! But in the logic of necessity there's no room for God: you *must* do, *must* do, *must* . . . They've become rule-bound. They are men with good manners but bad habits. Jesus calls them 'whited sepulchers.' That's the Lord's pain, God's pain, God's lament.

'Come and worship the Lord because he loves us.' 'Turn back to me with your whole heart,' he says, 'because I am kind and merciful.' Those who justify themselves don't understand mercy or kindness. But those people whom Jesus loved so much needed mercy and kindness and went to ask for it from the Lord.

In this time of Lent it will do all of us good to think about the Lord's invitation to love, to engage in that dialectic of freedom where love lies. It will do all of us good to ask ourselves: Is that the way I'm going? Or am I in danger of justifying myself and going a different way? On a road to nowhere because it leads to no promise? Let us pray to the Lord to give us the grace always to go the way of salvation, to open ourselves to salvation which comes from God alone, from faith, not from what those 'doctors of duty' proposed, who had lost faith and ruled the people by their theology of duty. Let us ask for this grace: Lord, give me the grace to open up to your salvation. That's what Lent's for. God loves us all: he loves us all! Let's make the effort to open up; that's all he asks. 'Open the door. I'll do the rest.' Let's allow him into ourselves, let him touch us tenderly and give us salvation. Amen.

GOING HOME

Friday, March 28, 2014
HOSEA 14:2-10; MARK 12:28-34

"If you want to know a father's tenderness, try turning to God: try and then tell me!" That was the spiritual advice suggested by Pope Francis during the Mass celebrated on Friday morning, March 28, in the chapel of St. Martha's Guest House. However many sins we may have committed, said the pope, God always awaits us and is ready to welcome us and to give us a homecoming party. He's a father who never tires of forgiving and doesn't check whether the final "balance" is negative: God can do nothing but love.

That attitude, explained the pope, is described well in the first reading in today's liturgy, taken from the book of Hosea (14:2-10). It's a text that "speaks to us of the God our Father's longing for all of us who have gone far away and distanced ourselves from him." And yet "how tenderly he speaks to us!"

Hosea writes: "Thus says the Lord: Return, O Israel, to the Lord." Yes, "come home!" The pope stressed the Father's tenderness: "Perhaps when we hear the word inviting us to conversion—be converted—it sounds a bit strong to us because it's telling us to change our lives. That's true." But the word conversion contains "God's tender longing." It's the passionate word of a "Father who says to his child: come back, come back; it's time to come home!"

"With this word alone we can spend so many hours in prayer," said the pope, noting how "God never tires": we see him over "many centuries" and "with so many apostasies of his people." Yet, "he always returns, because our God is a God who awaits us." So even "Adam left paradise with a punishment and a promise. The Lord is faithful to his promise because he cannot deny himself: he's faithful!"

So "God has awaited all of us, throughout history." Indeed "he's a God who always awaits us." The pope invited us to contemplate "that beautiful image of the father and the prodigal son." Luke's gospel (15:11-32) "tells us that the father sees his son in the distance because he was looking out to see whether his son would come back." So the father was awaiting his son's return and "when he sees him coming he rushes out and puts his arms round him." Perhaps on the way the son had prepared what he would say when he got home: "Father, I have sinned against heaven and before you. I am no longer worthy to be called your son." But "his father didn't let him speak" and "shut his mouth with a kiss."

Jesus' parable makes us understand who "our father is: God who always awaits us." Someone might say: "But, Father, I have so many sins that I don't know whether he'll be happy with me!" The pope's answer was: "Give it a try! If you want to know this Father's tenderness, go to him and give it a try! Then come and tell me!" Because "the God who awaits us is also the God who forgives: it's we who grow tired of asking for forgiveness. But he never tires: seventy times seven! Always! On with forgiveness!"

Of course, continued the pope, "from a business viewpoint the balance is negative, that's true! He always loses, he loses out on the balance. But he wins in love because he—we can say this—is the first one to fulfill the commandment of love: he loves, he can't do anything else!" And we hear this in today's gospel passage (Mark 12:28-34).

As we read in the book of Hosea today, he's a God who tells us: "I will heal you, for my anger has turned from you." That's the way God speaks: "I call you in order to heal you!" So, explained the pope, "the miracles that Jesus did, healing so many sick people, were also a sign of the great miracle that the Lord does every day with us, when we have the courage to get up and go to him."

God who awaits and forgives us is also "the God who gives a party." Not by organizing a banquet like "that rich man with poor Lazarus lying at his gate. No, that's not the kind of party God likes," declared the Holy Father. Instead, God prepares "another feast, like the father of the prodigal son." In the text from Hosea, he explained, God tells us: "you will blossom like the lily." His promise is: I'll give a party for you. So "your shoots will spread out, your beauty will be like the olive tree and your fragrance like that of Lebanon."

Pope Francis concluded his meditation by stressing again that "each person's life, each man's, each woman's who has the courage to approach the Lord will encounter the joy of God's banquet." Hence his final prayer: "May this word help us to think about our Father, the Father who always awaits us, who always forgives us, and who gives a party when we come home!"

DON'T BE LIFE-STYLE TOURISTS

Monday, March 31, 2014
ISAIAH 65:17-21; JOHN 4:43-54

Neither "drifting Christians like life-style tourists" nor "static Christians but witnesses to "a faith on the move," following God's promises. That's the Christian identity described by Pope Francis this morning, Monday, March 31, during the Mass celebrated in the chapel of St. Martha's Guest House.

The pope spoke about the value in a Christian's life of faith in Jesus who "never disappoints us." It's written in the gospel and Pope Francis stressed it, commenting on the readings in the day's liturgy. "In the first reading," he began, quoting Isaiah (65:17-21), "we hear God's promise of what awaits us. What God has prepared for us: 'I am creating new heavens and a new Earth . . .' The past, with all its troubles, will no longer be remembered . . . everything will be new. 'I am creating Jerusalem as a joy . . .' There will be joy. It's the promise of joy."

Before asking for anything, explained the bishop of Rome, the Lord makes a promise. So the bedrock of the virtue of hope is trusting in the Lord's promises. "This hope doesn't disappoint," the pope declared, "because God is faithful and doesn't disappoint." The Lord, he continued, always makes a promise first, before telling anyone to go ahead. "Even Adam," he recalled, "when he was driven out of paradise, was given one." That "is our destiny: to walk within sight of the promises, certain that they will become reality. It's beautiful to read chapter 11 of the Letter to the Hebrews, which tells of the journey of the people of God toward the promises: how those people loved those promises and pursued them even to martyrdom. They knew the Lord was faithful. That hope never disappoints."

To help us realize the value of trusting in the Father's promises, the pope referred to the episode in John's gospel (4:43-54), which had just been read. It tells the story of the royal official who heard that Jesus had come to Cana and went to meet him to beg him to save his sick son, who was lying near death at Capernaum. It was enough, the pope recalled, for Jesus to say, "Go, your son will live," for that man to believe his words and set out on his journey: "That's our life: to believe and set out on our journey," as Abraham did, who "trusted in the Lord and went ahead even when times were difficult," when, for example, his faith "was tested because he was asked to sacrifice his son." Even then, "he went on. He trusted in the Lord," stressed the pope, "and carried on. Christian life's like that: journeying toward the promises." So "Christian life is hope."

However, we can also not progress in life. "In fact," noted the bishop of Rome, "so many people, even Christians, Catholics, don't make the journey. There's the temptation to stand still," to think you're a good Christian, just because you are a member of a church and feel as if you are in your own "spiritual home," as if you were too "tired" to go ahead.

"We have so many static Christians. Their hope is weak. Yes, they believe in heaven but they don't seek it. They keep the commandments, all the regulations, everything," noted the pope, but they're static. The Lord can't draw yeast from them to make his people grow. That's a problem: those who are stuck."

"Then," he added, "there are others, who have lost their way. We all lose our way sometimes." But the problem, he said, "isn't losing your way. The problem is not turning back when you realize you have. It's our sinful state that makes us lose our way. We carry on, but sometimes we make a mistake and lose our way. But we can turn back: the Lord gives us this grace, of being able to turn back."

Then "there's another group, which is more dangerous," he said, "because they deceive themselves." They are "those who journey but get nowhere. They are drifting Christians: they drift about in a kind of life-style tourism, with no goal, without taking the promises seriously. These drifters are deceiving themselves because they say: 'I'm moving on . . .' No, you're not moving on, you're drifting! But the Lord asks us not to stop, not to lose our way, and not to drift through life. He asks us to look to the promises, to go ahead seeking the promises," like the man in John's gospel, who "believed in Jesus' promises and set out on his journey." For faith sets out on the journey.

Lent, he said in conclusion, is a good time to consider where we are on the journey or whether we are "too static"—and need to change. Or whether "we have lost our way"—and need to go to confession "to get back on the right road." Or last, whether we are "theological tourists," like those who drift through life "but never take a step forward."

Pope Francis' final exhortation was: "Let us ask the Lord for the grace to get back on the journey and carry on toward the promises. While we are thinking about this, it will do us good to reread chapter 11 of the Letter to the Hebrews, to understand what it means to journey toward the promises the Lord has made to us."

BEYOND THE FORMALITIES

Tuesday, April 1, 2014
JOHN 5:1-16

We should approach all the wounded in that great "field hospital which is a symbol of the church" without spiritual sloth or *acedia* and without formalities. That's what Pope Francis recommended in the Mass celebrated on Tuesday morning, April 1, in the chapel of St. Martha's Guest House. He also invited Christians "not to live under an anesthetic" and to overcome the temptation "to gloom and resignation" and the temptation "not to get involved."

"In today's liturgy," he explained, commenting on the readings, "water is a symbol, healing water, water that brings health." He referred especially to the passage from John's gospel (5:1-16). It's "the story of that man, who had been paralyzed for thirty-eight years" and lay, together with so many other sick people, near the pool in Jerusalem, hoping to be healed. Then when "Jesus saw the man, he asked him: do you want to be cured?" The man replied at once: "'Of course I do, Lord! But I have no one to put me into the pool when the water is stirred up. And while I'm making my way, someone else steps down ahead of me.'" For "they had the idea," explained the pope, "that when the waters became stirred up it was the angel of the Lord coming to cure them." Jesus' answer was an order: "Stand up, take your mat and walk!" And the man was cured.

Then, the pope continued, "the apostle changes the tone of the story and recalls that that day was the Sabbath." So he reports the reactions of those who rebuked the healed man for carrying his mat on the Sabbath day, which was forbidden. That attitude, said the pope, reminds us "of our own behavior in the face of so many physical and spiritual sicknesses people have." In particular, he noted, "I find here" the image "of two severe spiritual sicknesses" which it will "do us good to reflect on a bit."

The "first sickness" is the one afflicting the paralyzed man who "had become resigned" and maybe said to himself: "'Life's unfair; other people are luckier than me!'" His way of talking "is a gentle whine: he's resigned but also embittered." That attitude, said the pope, also makes us think "of so many joyless and embittered Catholics," who tell themselves: "'I go to Mass every Sunday but it's better not to become too involved! I have faith in my own salvation but I don't feel the need to pass it on to anyone else: each to his own, with no fuss,'" also because "if you do anything in life, you get told off: better not to risk it!"

This is "the sickness of *acedia* in Christians," an "attitude that paralyzes apostolic zeal" and "makes Christians become static, calm, but not in the good sense of the word: people who don't bother to go out and proclaim the gospel. People who have been anesthetized." A spiritual anesthesia which leads them to think "negatively, that it's better not to become involved," to live "with that spiritual *acedia*. And *acedia* is sadness." It's the description of "Christians who are habitually gloomy," who enjoy savoring their sadness until they become "gloomy and negative." That, warned the pope, "is a sickness for us Christians." Perhaps "we go to Mass every Sunday," but we also say: "please don't disturb!" Christians "without apostolic zeal are of no use and they do the church no good." Unfortunately, said the pope, today there are so many "selfish Christians," who commit "the sin of *acedia* against apostolic zeal, against the will to give the newness of Jesus to others; that newness which was freely given to me."

The other sin mentioned today by the pope was the "formalism" of the Jews. They get angry with the man who has just been healed by Jesus because he's carrying his mat on the Sabbath. They don't care that he's happy, even "dancing in the street" because he's finally free "of his physical sickness and also of his *acedia*, his sadness." The Jews' response is sharp: "Things aren't like that here, you've got to do this!" They were "only interested in the formalities: it was the Sabbath and you can't do miracles on the Sabbath!" It's the same attitude as that of those "hypocritical Christians who leave no room for God's grace." Because "for these people Christian life means having all your papers in order, all your documents!" But by doing this "they shut the door on God's grace." And, he added, "We have so many of them in the church!"

So here are the two sins. On the one hand there are "those who commit the sin of *acedia*," because "they're not capable of carrying on with their apostolic zeal and have decided to shut themselves up within themselves, in their own sadness and resentment!" On the other hand, there are those "who are incapable of bringing salvation because they close the door" and are only concerned "with formalities" to the point where "thou shalt not!" are the words they use most often.

"We also suffer from these two temptations and we ought to be aware of them in order to defend ourselves against them." In that "field hospital, which is a symbol of the church today, with so many wounded people," Jesus certainly doesn't give in to these temptations to *acedia* or formalism. But "he approaches that man and asks him: 'Do you want to be cured?'" To the man who just says yes, "he gives grace and then goes on his way." Jesus, explained the pope, "doesn't sort out his life: he gives him grace and grace does it all!" Then, the gospel tells us, when he meets that man again later in the temple, he says something else to him: "'Look, you're cured, so don't sin anymore!'" Those, declared the pope, are "two Christian words: 'do you want to be cured?' and 'don't sin anymore!'" First, Jesus heals the sick man and then he invites him "not to sin anymore." That's "the Christian way, the way of apostolic zeal," to "approach many of the wounded in this field hospital. Indeed, often some of them are wounded by men and women of the church." So we need to talk like a brother or sister, inviting them first to be cured and then "not to sin anymore." Without any doubt, the pope concluded, these "two words of Jesus are far better than the attitude of *acedia* or the attitude of hypocrisy."

A Friend to Pray With

Thursday, April 3, 2014
Exodus 32:7-14

Praying is like talking to a friend: so "prayer must be free, brave, insistent," even to the point of reproaching the Lord.

Realizing that the Holy Spirit is always there and teaches us what to do. That's the way Moses prayed, said Pope Francis during the Mass celebrated on Thursday morning, April 3, in the chapel of St. Martha's Guest House.

This small prayer manual was suggested to the pope by the reading of the passage from the book of Exodus (32:7-14). It relates "Moses' prayer for his people, who had fallen into the very grave sin of idolatry." "The Lord," explained the pope, "rebukes Moses," and tells him: "Go down at once! Your people, whom you brought up out of the land of Egypt, have acted perversely."

It's as if in this conversation God wanted to distance himself, telling Moses: "I've got nothing to do with this people; they are yours, they are no longer my people." But Moses replies: "O Lord, why does your wrath burn hot against your people, whom you brought out of the land of Egypt with great power and with a mighty hand?" Thus, declared the Holy Father, "it's as if the people were between two masters, two fathers: people of God and people of Moses."

So then Moses begins his prayer, "a real struggle with God." It's "the struggle of the people's leader to save his people, who are the people of God." Moses "speaks freely to the Lord." By doing so, "he teaches us how to pray: without fear, freely, and also insistently." Moses "insists, he's brave: prayer must be like that!"

Just saying words and nothing else isn't praying. You also have to know how to negotiate with God. Just as "Moses does, reminding God, by arguments, of the relationship he has with his people." He "tries to convince God" that if he unleashes his anger against the people he will "lose face before all the Egyptians." Indeed, in the book of Exodus we read these words of Moses to God: "Why should the Egyptians say: 'It was with evil intent that he brought them out to kill them in the mountains and to consume them from the face of the earth?' Turn from your fierce wrath; change your mind and don't bring disaster on your people."

Moses "tries to convince God to change his mind by arguing with him. The arguments he uses are from memories." So "he tells God: you've done this and this and this for your people, but if you now let them die in the wilderness, what will our enemies say?" They will say "that you are evil, that you are not faithful." In this way Moses "tries to convince the Lord," by engaging in a struggle, in which he focuses upon two elements: "your people and my people."

His prayer is successful, because "in the end Moses manages to convince the Lord." The pope remarked that "it's lovely the way this passage finishes": "The Lord changed his mind about the disaster he planned to bring on his people." Certainly, he explained, "the Lord was getting rather tired of this unfaithful people." But "when we read at the end of the passage that the Lord changed his mind" we should ask ourselves a question: Who was it who really changed his mind? Did the Lord change his? "I believe not," the bishop of Rome replied. It was Moses who changed his, because, said the pope, he believed that the Lord was going to destroy the people. And "he searches in his memory to remember how kind the Lord had been with his people, how he had delivered them from slavery in Egypt to lead them forward with a promise."

It is "by these arguments that he tries to convince God. In the process he rediscovers the memory of his people and God's mercy." Actually, the pope continued, "Moses is afraid that God will do that terrible thing." But "in the end he goes down the mountain" with a great awareness in his heart: "our God is merciful, he can forgive, he can revoke his decisions, he's a father!"

These are all things that Moses already "knew, but knew in a vague sort of way. He rediscovers them in prayer." That's also what "prayer does in us: it changes our hearts, it makes us understand better what our God is like." But for this to happen, added the pope, "it's important not to speak to the Lord with empty words, as the pagans do." Instead, we need to speak out plainly: "'Look, Lord, I've got this problem in my family, with my child, with this or that person . . . What can be done? Look, you can't leave me like this!'"

Prayer takes time. In fact "praying is also negotiating with God to get what I'm asking him for," but above all to know him better. Prayer must be "like a friend talking with a friend." Moreover, "the Bible tells us that Moses spoke to the Lord face to face, like a friend." For "that's how prayer should be: free, insistent, using arguments." Even "'reproaching' the Lord somewhat: but you promised me this and you haven't done it!" It's like "talking with a friend: prayer means opening our hearts."

Pope Francis recalled that after his face to face with God, "Moses came down the mountain reinvigorated. He had learned to know the Lord better. With the strength he had received from him he resumed his work of leading the people toward the promised land." So prayer reinvigorates.

The pope concluded by asking the Lord "to give us all grace, because praying is a grace." He invited us to always to remember that "when we pray to God, it's not just a conversation between two," because "in every prayer there's always the Holy Spirit." So "we can't pray without the Holy Spirit: it's he who prays in us, it's he who changes our hearts, it's he who teaches us to call God 'Father.'"

And, the pope added, we should ask the Holy Spirit to teach us to pray "as Moses prayed, to negotiate with God freely and bravely." And "may the Holy Spirit who is always present in our prayer lead us on this way."

WHERE IT'S FORBIDDEN TO PRAY

Friday, April 4, 2014
WISDOM 2:1, 12-22; JOHN 7:1-2, 10, 25-30

More Christians are martyred and persecuted today than in the early days of the church. To the point where in some countries it's even forbidden to pray together. It was on that dramatic fact that Pope Francis focused his meditation during the Mass celebrated on Friday morning, April 4, in the chapel of St. Martha's Guest House.

The passage from the book of Wisdom (2:1, 12-22), read in the day's liturgy, reveals "how the hearts of the ungodly, people who have gone far from God, have taken over religion." And "how they behave towards the prophets," even persecuting them. These people, said the pope, knew perfectly well that they are dealing with a good man. Scripture describes how they think: "Let us lie in wait for the righteous man, because he's inconvenient to us and opposes our actions."

Lying in wait, explained the pope, means "promoting gossip among themselves, telling lies." Thus they slander him "and lay a trap to destroy the good man." Indeed, the Old Testament tells us, they can't accept that the righteous man "opposes our actions, reproaches us for transgressions against the law, and accuses us of sins against our training."

These words describe the prophets who are persecuted "throughout salvation history." Jesus himself said so to the Pharisees, the pope recalled, as we hear in "that famous chapter 23 of Matthew's gospel, which it will do us good to read." Jesus is outspoken. "Your fathers, he says, killed the prophets, but in order to relieve your guilt, to cleanse yourselves, you build them a fine tomb!"

Here, said the Holy Father, "we have historical hypocrisy." It's a fact that "throughout salvation history, during Israel's time and the time of the church, the prophets have been persecuted." For the prophet is a man "who says: but you are going wrong, turn back to God! That's the message of a prophet." A message "that doesn't please those who are in charge of that wrong way."

Jesus was also persecuted. They wanted to kill him, as we read in today's gospel (John 7:1-2, 10, 25-30). He certainly "knew what his end would be." The persecution began at once when "at the beginning of his ministry he returned to his own town and went into the synagogue to preach." Then, "at first they were amazed but immediately they began" murmuring, as the gospel tells us: "We know where this man is from; but when the Messiah comes no one will know where he comes from." They all ask: "By what authority do you come to teach us? Where did you study?"

In a word, it's the same attitude as always: "They discredit the Lord, they discredit the prophet in order to remove his authority." It's like saying, "This man does miracles on the Sabbath, but it's forbidden to work on the Sabbath, so he must be a sinner! This man eats, he goes to dinner with sinners and so he's not a man of God!" Thus "they discredit Jesus," because "he moved out and made others move out from that closed religious atmosphere, that prison." And "the prophet fights against people who imprison the Holy Spirit." For that reason "he's always persecuted." The prophets "are all persecuted, misunderstood, sidelined; they are not accepted." That's a reality "which didn't end with the death and resurrection of Jesus" but which "has continued in the church."

Indeed, in the church they have been "persecuted from outside and persecuted from within." The saints themselves "have been persecuted." In fact, noted the bishop of Rome, "when we read the lives of the saints," we find so much "misunderstanding and persecution." Because, as they were prophets, they said things which people found "too hard."

Even "so many thinkers in the church have been persecuted." Pope Francis made the point: "I'm thinking of someone now, at this moment, not very far from us: a man of good will, a real prophet, who rebuked the church in his books for turning away from the Lord. He was immediately summoned, his books were put on the index, they removed him from office and that's how that man's life ended not so long ago. Now time has passed and today he's been beatified." But someone might object, how come "yesterday he was a heretic and now he's been beatified?" Yes, "yesterday those who were in power wanted to silence him because they didn't like what he was saying. But today, thanks be to God, the church has repented and said: no, he was a good man! What's more: he's on the road to sainthood: he's been beatified."

So history tells us that "everyone chosen by the Holy Spirit to speak the truth to the people of God suffers persecution." The pope recalled "the last of Jesus' beatitudes: Blessed are you when you are persecuted in my name." Here "Jesus himself is the model, the image: the Lord suffered so much, he was persecuted" and thereby "took on all the persecutions of his people."

But "Christians are still being persecuted today," warned the pope. To the point where "I make bold to say that there are as many or more martyrs now than in the early church." They are persecuted "because they tell the truth to this worldly society, this tranquil society that doesn't want problems, and they proclaim Jesus Christ." Indeed, "today there is so much persecution."

Today in some places "there's the death penalty, imprisonment for possessing a Gospel at home, for teaching the catechism," stressed the pope and added: "A Catholic told me about these countries where they can't even pray together: it's forbidden. You can only pray alone and in secret." If they want to celebrate the Eucharist they organize "a birthday party, they pretend they are celebrating a birthday and they do! First the Eucharist then the party." If, as "has happened, they see the police arriving, at once they hide everything and go on with the party" with "congratulations and good wishes." Then when the police "have gone, they finish the Eucharist." They "have to do that because it's forbidden to pray together."

Actually, remarked the pope, "that history of persecution and misunderstanding" has been continual "from the time of the prophets up until today." After all, it's also "the way of the Lord, the way of those who follow the Lord." A way that "always ends, as it did for the Lord, with a resurrection, but which comes after the crucifixion." So the pope recommended that we "not be afraid of persecution or misunderstanding," even if through them "so many things are always lost."

For Christians "there will always be persecution, misunderstanding." But we have to face them in the certainty that "Jesus is the Lord and that's the challenge and the cross of our faith." So, the Holy Father recommended, "when these things happen in our communities or in our hearts, let us look to the Lord and think" of the passage from the book of Wisdom, which speaks of the ungodly lying in wait for the righteous. He concluded by asking the Lord "for the grace to keep going his way—even, should that happen, when it's the way of the cross and persecution."

Forgiveness with a Loving Touch

Monday, April 7, 2014
John 8:1-11

"God forgives not by a decree but with a loving touch." And with mercy. "Jesus also goes beyond the law and forgives by gently stroking our sins' bruises." During the Mass celebrated on Monday, April 7, in the chapel of St. Martha's Guest House, Pope Francis devoted his homily to God's tenderness.

"Today's readings," explained the pope, "speak to us about

adultery" which, together with blasphemy and idolatry, was considered "a very grave sin in the Mosaic law," punished by "the death penalty," by stoning. Actually, adultery "goes against the image of God, God's faithfulness," because "marriage is the symbol of God's faithful relationship with his people and also a human reality embodying it." So "when marriage is damaged by adultery, that relationship between God and his people is blemished." At the time it was considered to be "a grave sin," because "it blemished the symbol of God's relationship with his people, God's faithfulness."

In today's gospel passage (John 8:1-11), which tells the story of the woman caught in adultery, "we meet Jesus sitting among a crowd of people and teaching." Then "the scribes and Pharisees approached pushing forward a woman—we can imagine that perhaps her hands were bound." So "they stood her in front of him and accused her: she's an adulteress!" That was "a public accusation." The gospel tells us, they put the question to Jesus: "What should we do with this woman? You speak to us about kindness but Moses said we should kill her!" They "said this," noted the pope, "to put him to the test, so that they could accuse him." For "if Jesus said yes, go ahead and stone her," they would be able to say to the people: "Look at your teacher, who's so kind. Look what he's done to this poor woman!" But if "Jesus said no, forgive the poor woman!" then they could accuse him "of not keeping the law."

Their single aim was "to put Jesus to the test and trap him." For "they were not concerned about the woman; they weren't bothered about adultery." And "perhaps some of them were even adulterers themselves."

Although he was among so many people, "Jesus wanted to be alone with the woman; he wanted to speak with her heart to heart: that's the most important thing for Jesus." Then "the people went away slowly" after they had heard his words: "Let anyone among you who is without sin be the first to throw a stone at her."

"With a certain irony the gospel tells us that they all sloped off, one by one, beginning with the eldest," commented the bishop of Rome. "We can see that their account with the bank of heaven was well overdrawn!" So now we have "the moment when Jesus becomes her confessor." He is left "alone with the woman," who remains "standing there." Meanwhile, "Jesus was bending down and writing with his finger in the dust. Some exegetes say that he was writing down the sins of those scribes and Pharisees. Perhaps that's just imagination." Then he "straightened up and looked" at the woman, who was "filled with shame, and he said to her: 'Woman, where are they? Has no one condemned you? We are alone, you and I. You are standing before God. With no one to accuse you, no one to speak against you: you and God.'"

The woman doesn't claim to be the victim of "a false accusation." She doesn't defend herself by saying, "I haven't committed adultery." No, "she recognizes her sin" and answers Jesus, "No one, sir. No one has condemned me." In his turn Jesus tells her: "Neither do I condemn you. Go and from now on sin no more, so that you don't go through such another hard time, or suffer such shame again, so that you don't offend God or spoil the beautiful relationship between God and his people."

"Jesus forgives her. But here we have something more than forgiveness. As a confessor, Jesus goes beyond the law." Indeed, "the law said she should be punished." What's more, Jesus "was pure and could have thrown the first stone." But he "goes further. He doesn't tell her, adultery isn't a sin. But he doesn't condemn her by the law." So "that's the mystery of Jesus' mercy."

Thus "in order to be merciful," Jesus goes beyond "the law that commanded she should be stoned." He tells the woman to go in peace. "Mercy," explained the pope, "is a difficult thing to understand; it doesn't wipe out the sins," because what wipes out the sins "is God's forgiveness." But "mercy is the way in which God forgives." For "Jesus could have said: I forgive you, go! As he said to the paralyzed man: your sins are forgiven you!" But in this situation "Jesus goes further" and advises the woman "to sin no more." And "here we see Jesus' merciful attitude: he defends the sinner from her enemies, defends the sinner from her just condemnation."

"That also applies to us," added the pope. "How many of us perhaps deserve to be condemned. The condemnation would also be just. But he forgives!" How? "By that mercy," which "doesn't wipe out the sin: it's God's forgiveness that wipes it out," whereas "mercy goes further." It's "like looking up at the sky, with so many stars, but when the sun rises in the morning, it's so bright that the stars can no longer be seen." And "that's what God's mercy is like: a shining light of love, of tenderness." For "God doesn't forgive by a decree, but with a loving touch." He does so by "gently stroking the bruises of our sins, because he's involved in forgiveness, involved in our salvation."

That's the way, Pope Francis concluded, "Jesus behaves as a confessor." He doesn't humiliate the woman caught in adultery, "he doesn't ask: what did you do? When? Who with?" Instead he tells her "to go and sin no more. God's mercy is great, Jesus' mercy is great: forgiving us with a loving touch."

The Dictatorship of a Single Way of Thinking

Thursday, April 10, 2014
Genesis 17:3-9; John 8:51-59

"Today too we find the dictatorship of a single way of thinking." If you don't think in a particular way, you're not considered to be modern or open-minded. And worse still is "when certain rulers ask for financial support" and they get the answer "but if you want this support you must think like this and pass this law and that." The risk of a single way of thinking threatening our relationship with God was the focus of Pope Francis' homily during the Mass celebrated on Thursday morning, April 10, at St. Martha's. "The phenomenon of a single way of thinking" has always caused "misfortunes in the history of humanity," declared the Holy Father, recalling the tragedies of the twentieth century. But, he said, we can resist: by praying and keeping watch.

Turning to the day's readings, the pope stressed how the liturgy "makes us see God's promise to our father Abraham." He was referring to the passage from Genesis (17:3-9), in which God promises Abraham that he will become "the father of a multitude of nations." "From that moment on," explained the Holy Father, "the people of God began on their journey seeking" the fulfillment of this promise, so that it became reality. It's "a promise which takes the form of a covenant between Abraham and God." God tells Abraham: "As for you, you shall keep my covenant, you and your descendants after you throughout their generations." So "the covenant must be kept."

Thus, the pope continued, "we understand that the commandments are not a rigid law; the commandments arose from this loving relationship, this promise, this covenant." Taking his cue from the passage from John's gospel (8:51-59), read in the liturgy of the day, the pope continued his reflection, saying, "the mistake made by those doctors of the law who were not good and wanted to stone Jesus—however, there were also good Pharisees and doctors of the law in those days—was to separate the commandments from the promise, the covenant." That means "separating the commandments from the heart of God, who commanded Abraham always to journey on."

For Pope Francis, "the mistake, the error of those people," arose from their not having "understood the way of hope: they believed that with the commandments everything was done, complete." But "the commandments, which arose from love of God's faithfulness, are rules for carrying on, indications of how to proceed. They help us to walk on and complete our encounter with Jesus." But "those people about whom the gospel is speaking today didn't know how to link fulfillment of the commandments to God's covenant with their ancestor Abraham." They kept repeating: "These are laws that we must keep!" They did so because "their hearts were closed, their minds were closed, to anything new and also to what the prophets had promised." For them all that counted was "we've got to do this and proceed like that!"

That, noted the pope, "is the story of the closed heart, the story of the closed mind. When the heart is closed, that closes the mind. When heart and mind are closed, there's no room for God." Yes, explained the pope, then we are "on our own" and also convinced that "we ought to do only what we believe," and feel sure that we're doing exactly "what the commandments tell us." But "the commandments bear a promise and the prophets awaken that promise."

When faced with "a closed mind, Jesus found it impossible to convince, impossible to give a message of something new." Something which is, nevertheless, "not new" but "what was promised by God's faithfulness and by the prophets." Yet those challenging Jesus "didn't understand, their minds were closed, their thinking was blinkered, because by their selfishness, by their sins they had closed off their own hearts." So "their thinking is blinkered, not open to dialogue, to the possibility of something else, the possibility that God might speak to us and tell us his way, as he did to the prophets." Surely, added the pope, "these people hadn't listened to the prophets and they didn't listen to Jesus." But their behavior "is more than just stubbornness. No, it's more than that! It's worship of their own way of thinking: 'I think this, it has to be just like this and nothing else!'"

The Pharisees presented in today's gospel passage "had a single way of thinking and wanted to impose it on the people of God. That's why Jesus reproached them for laying so many commandments on the people's shoulders. He reproached them for their inconsistency," caused by their thinking "it has to be done this way!" Thus they had a "theology in thrall to that single way of thinking." In the end "dialogue becomes impossible, and it becomes impossible to open up to the newness God brings with the prophets." After all, these people "killed the prophets" and "shut the door on God's promise."

The "phenomenon of a single way of thinking" has always "caused misfortunes in the history of humanity," declared the pope. "During the last century we all saw the dictatorships of a single way of thinking that ended up killing so many people." They felt they were the masters and "you couldn't think differently: there's just one way of thinking!"

But "even today," warned the pope, "there is worship of a single way of thinking. Today you have to think like this and if you don't you aren't modern, you're not open-minded." Worse still is "when certain rulers ask for financial support" and they get the answer, "but if you want this support you must think like this and pass this law and that one and that one."

So "even today we find the dictatorship of a single way of thinking and that dictatorship is the same as those people's" in the gospel story. The way of behaving is the same. These are people "who take up stones to stone freedom, a country's freedom, freedom of conscience, people's freedom, their relationship with God. Today Jesus is crucified again."

Thus, continued the pope, "this is not just a story about bad Pharisees with closed minds in the past—there were also good Pharisees. It's also a story about today." And "the Lord's advice for that kind of dictatorship is the same as ever: watch and pray."

The pope concluded by urging us "not to be stupid," not to buy things that are of no use. And "to be humble and pray that the Lord may always give us the freedom of an open heart to receive his word, which is a promise and a joy! A covenant! And to carry on with that covenant."

DEFINITELY THE DEVIL

Friday, April 11, 2014
JOHN 10:31-42

"The devil is also here in the twenty-first century and we need to learn from the gospel how to fight against him," so that we don't fall into his trap. However, to do so we mustn't be "naïve." We need to know his strategies for tempting us, which always have "three characteristics": they begin quietly, then they grow through contamination, and finally they find a way of justifying themselves. Pope Francis warned us against thinking that talk of the devil today is "old-fashioned." This was the focus of his meditation at the Mass celebrated on Friday, April 11, in the chapel of St. Martha's Guest House.

The pope spoke expressly of a "struggle." After all, he explained, "Jesus' life was also a struggle: he came to defeat evil, to defeat the prince of this world, to defeat the devil." Jesus fought with the devil who tempted him so many times and "in his life he suffered temptations and also persecutions." So "even we Christians who want to follow Jesus, and who through baptism are on the way of Jesus, must understand this truth well: we too are tempted, we too are attacked by the devil." That happens, "because the spirit of evil doesn't want us to be holy, doesn't want our Christian witness, doesn't want us to be disciples of Jesus."

But, asked the pope, "what does the spirit of evil do to tempt us from the way of Jesus?" His answer to that question was clear.

"The devil's temptation," explained the pope, "has three characteristics and we need to know them, so that we don't fall into the trap." First, "temptation starts quietly, but then grows; it always grows." Then "it contaminates someone else"; it's "carried to someone else and tries to become communal." And "finally, to calm our soul it justifies itself." So the characteristics of temptation can be summed up in three words: it "grows, contaminates, and justifies" itself.

We also find this in "the first temptation of Jesus" in the wilderness, which "seems almost like a seduction. The devil goes slowly" and says to Jesus: "But why don't you do this? Throw yourself down from the temple and you'll save thirty years of life; in one day everyone will be saying, 'Here's the Messiah!'" It's the same thing "that he did with Adam and Eve." The devil says to them: "Taste this apple; it's good, it will give you knowledge!" The devil uses the tactic of "seduction"; he speaks "almost as if he were a spiritual master, as if he were a counselor."

But "if the temptation is resisted," then "it grows and becomes stronger." Jesus, explained the pope, tells us so in Luke's gospel and warns us that "when the devil is driven out, he wanders around and finds some companions and returns with this gang." Thus "the temptation becomes stronger, it grows. But it also grows by involving others." That's just what happened with Jesus, as we hear in the passage from John's gospel (10:31-42) in today's liturgy. "The devil," declared the pope, "involves these enemies of Jesus who, at this point, are talking to him with stones in their hands," prepared to kill him. Here "we see very clearly how forcefully" temptation grows through contamination. So "what seemed like a little trickle of water, a gentle little trickle of water, becomes a tide, a strong river that carries you with it." Because temptation "always grows and contaminates others."

The third characteristic of temptation by the devil is that "finally, it justifies itself." Pope Francis recalled the people's reaction when Jesus returned "for the first time to his home in Nazareth" and went to the synagogue. First they were all struck by his words, then temptation arose. "But isn't this man the son of Joseph the carpenter, and of Mary? By what authority does he speak if he's never been to university and never studied?" Thus they tried to justify their plan to "kill him, throw him down from the cliff."

In the passage from John's gospel the people talking to Jesus also want to kill him; they even "have stones in their hands as they're arguing with him." Thus "temptation involved them all against Jesus"; and they all "justify themselves." For Pope Francis "the height of self-justification comes with the priest," who says: "Let's get rid of him; you don't understand anything! Don't you know it's better for one man to die for the people? He has to die to save the people!" And all the others agree with him: it's "total self-justification."

We too, warned the pope, "do the same thing when we're tempted. The temptation grows and contaminates others." Think only of gossip: if "we're a bit jealous of someone," we don't keep it to ourselves but we share it, and speak spitefully to others about him or her. Thus gossip "grows and contaminates one person and another and another." Indeed, "that's how gossip works and we've all been tempted to gossip." The pope recognized and confided: "I too have been tempted to gossip! It's an everyday temptation," which "begins gently, like a little trickle of water."

That's why, repeated the pope, we must "be on our guard when we feel in our hearts something that will end up destroying others, destroying a reputation, destroying our lives, leading us to worldliness, to sin." We must "be on our guard, because if we don't stop that little trickle in time, when it grows and takes in others, it will become a tide that will lead us to justify ourselves for the wrong we have done." Just as "those people justified themselves," whom we heard about in the gospel, who ended up saying about Jesus, "It's better that one man should die for the people."

"We are all tempted," declared the pope, "because the law of our spiritual life, our Christian life, is to struggle." The reason for that is that "the prince of this world doesn't want us to be holy, doesn't want us to follow Christ."

Of course, concluded the pope, "one of you—perhaps, I don't know—might say, but Father, you're so old-fashioned speaking about the devil in the twenty-first century!" But the pope repeated, "Look out, the devil exists! The devil also exists in the twenty-first century. We mustn't be naïve. We must learn from the gospel how to fight against him."

DON'T BE AFRAID OF JOY

Thursday, April 24, 2014
LUKE 24:35-48

There are so many Christians who are "afraid of joy." Pope Francis described them jokingly as "bat-Christians," who go about in the dark with "lugubrious faces," instead of making for "the light of the Lord's presence."

The pope's reflection during the Mass celebrated on Thursday, April 24, in the chapel of St. Martha's Guest House focused on the apostles' conflicting feelings after the Lord's resurrection. On the one hand, there was their joy at realizing he had risen again, and on the other, their fear of seeing him among them again, entering into real contact with his living mystery. Taking his cue from the day's gospel passage, from Luke (24:35-48), the pope recalled that "on the day of his resurrection, in the evening, the disciples were telling each other what they had seen." The two Emmaus disciples reported their meeting with Jesus along the way and Peter also told his story. So "they were all happy that the

Lord had risen again: they were certain the Lord had risen." But "as they were speaking," the gospel tells us, "Jesus himself stood in the midst of them" and greeted them saying: "Peace be with you!"

At that moment, noted the pope, what happened was the complete opposite of what might have been expected: not peace at all. Actually, the gospel describes the apostles as "startled and terrified." They "didn't know what to do and thought they were seeing a ghost." So, continued the pope, "Jesus had to tell them, but see, I'm not a ghost; touch me, look at my wounds!"

"There's a word in this gospel passage," said the Holy Father, "which explains very well what had happened at that moment." We read in the text: "they disbelieved for joy . . ." That's the point: the disciples "couldn't believe because they were afraid of joy." For "Jesus was bringing them joy: the joy of resurrection, the joy of his presence among them." But that very joy becomes "a hindrance to believing: they didn't believe for joy and were full of amazement."

Basically, the disciples "preferred to think that Jesus was an idea, a ghost, but not a reality." And "Jesus' whole task was to make them understand that he was real: 'Give me something to eat, touch me, it's me! A ghost doesn't have flesh, it's really me!'" Besides, added the pope, "remember that this was happening after some of them had seen him during the day: they were sure he was alive. Then we don't know what happened . . ."

The gospel passage suggests that "fear of joy is a Christian disease." We too "are afraid of joy" and we tell ourselves that "it's better to think, yes, God exists, but he's out there, Jesus is risen, he's out there!" As if to say: let's keep "our distance." And thus "we're afraid of Jesus coming too close, because that gives us joy."

That attitude also explains why there are "so many lugubrious Christians," whose "lives are like a continual funeral." Christians who "prefer gloom to joy: they'd rather go about in the dark than in the light of joy." Just "like those creatures," said the pope, "who only risk going out at night but do nothing in daylight. Like bats! Jokingly, we can call them 'bat-Christians,' who prefer the dark to the light of the Lord's presence."

"We're afraid of joy," continued the pope, "and by his resurrection Jesus gives us joy, the joy of being a Christian, the joy of following him closely, the joy of walking the way of the beatitudes, the joy of being with him." But, "so often we feel disturbed when that joy comes to us or we're afraid; or we think we're seeing a ghost or we think that Jesus is a way of behaving." So we tell ourselves: "But we're Christians so we must behave like this!" It matters little if Jesus is absent. But rather, we should ask ourselves: "But do you talk to Jesus? Do you say to him, 'Jesus, I believe you are alive, that you have risen, that you are close to me, that you won't abandon me?'" That "conversation with Jesus" is the real Christian life, realizing that "Jesus is always with us, always with our problems, our difficulties, our good works."

So, the pope reiterated, we must overcome "our fear of joy" and think how many times "we aren't joyful because we are afraid." Like the disciples who "were defeated" by the mystery of the cross. Hence their fear. "In my country," the pope added, "there's a saying: when you've burned yourself with boiling milk, afterwards you cry when you see a cow." So the disciples, "burned by the experience of the cross, said: no let's stop there! He's in heaven, that's wonderful; he's risen, but don't let him come back here again, we can't stand it!"

Pope Francis concluded his meditation by invoking the Lord to "do to us what he did to the disciples, who were afraid of joy: open our minds." In fact, we read in the gospel, "Then he opened their minds to understand the scriptures." So the pope's prayer was: "May the Lord open our minds and make us understand that he's a living reality, that he has a body, that he's with us and keeps us company, that he has won. Let us ask the Lord for the grace not to be afraid of joy."

THE CHRISTIAN COMMUNITY IN THREE BROAD BRUSHSTROKES

Tuesday, April 29, 2014
ACTS 4:32-37

Harmony, witness, and care for the needy: these are the "three brushstrokes" to paint the image of a Christian community. This community is the work of the Holy Spirit, modeled on that "people born from above," whose members "still didn't call themselves Christians," but who knew how to bear witness to Jesus Christ. That was the image presented by Pope Francis this Tuesday morning, April 29, during the Mass at St. Martha's. He was referring to a passage from the Acts of the Apostles (4:32). The whole of last week's liturgy focused on "being born from above." Today it offers us the image of "the community of new Christians," a "new-born people," whose members "still didn't call themselves Christians."

The pope spoke about what he called the "three brushstrokes," with which the liturgy shows us this image. "The whole group of those who believed were of one heart and soul; that's the first stroke." The second is that they were a group who "with great power bore witness to the Lord Jesus." The third is that "there was not a needy person among them."

These are the "three features," explained the Holy Father, "of that reborn people: harmony among themselves, peace; strong witness to the resurrection of Jesus Christ and to the poor." However, things "didn't always go like that," he added. In fact, after a time "internal disputes arose, doctrinal disputes, power struggles among them. Problems also arose in their relationship with the poor; the widows complained that they were not being helped properly." So there was no lack of difficulties.

Nevertheless, this image shows what "the way of life of a

Christian community" really should be, for those who believe in Jesus. First of all, noted Pope Francis, it's necessary to create an atmosphere in which there is "peace and harmony. 'They were of one heart and soul . . .' Peace, a community in peace. This means that in the community there's no room for gossip, envy, slander, or speaking ill of others," only for peace. Because "forgiveness and love reigned."

To check whether a Christian community lives up to this, said the pope, "we must ask ourselves, how do Christians behave? Are they gentle, humble? In that community are there power struggles among themselves, fights caused by envy? Is there gossip? Then that shows they are not on the way of Jesus Christ." For, in fact, in a community peace is "such an important feature. So important because the devil tries to divide us. Jesus shows us this way, the way of peace among us, love among us."

Moving on to the second feature of the image, the Holy Father invited us to ask ourselves if the Christian community "bears witness to the resurrection of Jesus Christ. Does this parish, this community, this diocese really believe that Jesus Christ is risen?" When the reply is not a decisive yes, "perhaps hearts are far" from that certainty. But we must "bear witness that Jesus is alive, among us." Only thus can we tell how a Christian community is faring.

Lastly, the pope spoke about the poor and the place they have among us. Here we need an examination of conscience which, he said, can be divided into two parts: "What is your attitude or this community's attitude to the poor?" Then: "Is this community poor? Poor in heart or poor in spirit? Or does it place its trust in wealth and power?"

In conclusion, the pope summed up the three features identifying a Christian community: "Harmony, witness, poverty, and taking care of the poor." "That's just what Jesus explained to Nicodemus," he said, stressing that it's all work of the Holy Spirit, "the only one who can make this happen." For "the Spirit creates the church. The Spirit creates unity; the Spirit urges you toward witness; the Spirit makes you poor because he is wealth; and he does so to enable you to care for the poor. That's why Jesus says, 'The wind blows where it will and you hear its sound but you don't know where it comes from or where it's going.' That's how anyone is who is born of the Spirit. We don't know how: the Spirit comes and goes, but it does these things."

The pope's final invitation was: "Let's think about our communities, our parishes, our movements, our colleges, our dioceses. It will do us good to take stock, asking, Is my community in peace and harmony or is it divided? Does my community bear witness to Jesus Christ or does it merely know intellectually that Christ is risen but does nothing about it, fails to proclaim it? Does my community take care of the poor? Is it a poor community?" And the pope's prayer was: "May the Holy Spirit help us to go this way, the way of all those who have been reborn by baptism."

People Are Still Being Killed in God's Name Today

Friday, May 2, 2014
Acts 5:34-42; John 6:1-15

Pope Francis wept at the news of Christians who had been crucified in recent days in a non-Christian country. He said this himself when he was celebrating Mass in the chapel of St. Martha's Guest House, on Friday morning, May 2. Today, he said, there are still people who try to control consciences and so "they kill and persecute in God's name." And there are Christians who, like the apostles, "rejoice to be considered worthy to suffer dishonor for the sake of the name of Jesus."

That "joy of Christian martyrs" is one of the "three images" presented by the pope. "Today," he declared, "there are so many martyrs. Consider that in some countries you can go to prison just for carrying the gospel! You can't wear a cross, you'll have to pay a fine! But your heart is glad." That's an image of the "joy of witness," which links the apostles with the martyrs of today. In his homily the pope spoke about the apostles' preaching, recalling that when they were arrested and flogged they were still glad to have borne witness to the Lord.

The other two images presented by the pope are of Jesus with all his love for the people and "the hypocrisy of the religious leaders with all their political maneuvers" to oppress the people.

The day's liturgical reading from John's gospel (6:1-15) tells us that "a large crowd" kept following Jesus, "because they saw the signs that he was performing for the sick and those possessed by demons." But they were also following him in order to listen to him, explained the pope, "because people were saying about him: this man speaks with authority! Not like those others, the doctors of the law, the Sadducees, all people who spoke but without authority." Actually, those were people "who didn't have a powerful way of speaking like Jesus." Powerful not because Jesus shouted: powerful in its gentleness, its love, in the loving way the Lord looked at people." The power was love: that was Jesus' authority and that's why "the people followed him."

This gospel passage, noted the pope, shows us "how much Jesus loves the people" and "thinks about them being hungry: 'These people here are hungry; how can we feed them?'" So "Jesus is concerned about the people's problems. It doesn't occur to him to do a head-count, but let's see how many there are following us, how the church grown." Jesus "speaks, preaches, loves, accompanies, goes along with people on their way." He is "gentle and humble." So "when the people are filled with enthusiasm at seeing someone so kind, who speaks with authority and loves them so much, they want to make him king, but he stops them. He tells them no, not that! And he goes off." Thus Jesus truly helped his people.

Then Pope Francis referred to the first reading, taken from the Acts of the Apostles (5:34-42), which shows us the disciples caught up "with problems of the Sanhedrin when the Sadducees have them arrested after the healing of a sick man." He recalled that, following the cure, "the high priest and all who were with him, that is, the sect of the Sadducees, were filled with jealousy. So they arrested the apostles and put them in the public prison." But "we know that the angel gets the apostles out of prison" and then they immediately go and teach in the temple. The reaction of the high priest and his party at that point is to have the apostles brought before the Sanhedrin.

"But," said the pope, "I'd like to dwell a bit on that word: jealousy." They were jealous because "they didn't tolerate people following Jesus. They couldn't bear it," and so "they were jealous." But that's "an ugly attitude," for jealousy turns to envy.

Nevertheless, he continued, "these people knew very well who Jesus was, they knew." Besides, "these were the same people who had paid the guards to say that the apostles had stolen Jesus' body. They had paid to silence the truth." And "when you pay to silence the truth, that's doing something very wrong." The ordinary people also knew who these leaders were and didn't follow them. Rather, "they put up with them because they had authority—the authority of the cult, the authority of religious discipline at that time, authority over them."

Nevertheless, "people followed Jesus," who plainly told the powerful that "they laid heavy burdens on the people and made them shoulder them." These powerful men wouldn't tolerate Jesus' gentleness, they wouldn't tolerate the gentleness of the gospel, they wouldn't tolerate love and repaid it with envy and hatred.

So here are "two images" to compare. The image of Jesus who was moved by the people because, says the gospel, he saw them as "sheep without a shepherd." Then "those with their political maneuvers, their religious maneuvers to continue dominating the people."

An attitude we find in the passage from the Acts of the Apostles: "Remember the apostles, whom they had flogged and ordered not to speak in the name of Jesus. Then they set them free." In short, said the pope, "they had to do something." So they decided, "We'll give them a good beating and then send them home."

They had committed an injustice, because they considered themselves to be "in charge of consciences" and "they felt they had the power to do it." What's more, added the pope, "in our world today there are also so many" who behave like that. That was when Pope Francis confided that he had wept at the news of "Christians crucified in a certain non-Christian country." Yes, he declared, "Today too there are people who kill and persecute in God's name." But today too there are people with the same attitude as the apostles—which we read about in Acts—"they rejoiced that they were considered worthy to suffer dishonor for the sake of the name of Jesus."

These are three images to keep well in mind, because they are important to the central question of "our salvation history." At the end of his reflection, Pope Francis reminded us of them again, showing "Jesus with the people," his love, which is "the way he has taught us" and "the way we must go." On the other hand, there is "the hypocrisy of those religious leaders who had imprisoned the people by so many commandments, with their cold, hard legality; and had also paid to silence the truth." Nevertheless, they still couldn't undermine "the joy of the Christian martyrs, the joy of so many brothers and sisters who throughout our history have felt that joy, that gladness to have been considered worthy to suffer dishonor for the sake of the name of Jesus."

Who Has a Place in the Church?

Monday, May 5, 2014
John 6:22-29

There's no place in the church for those who follow Jesus out of vanity, power seeking, or the desire for money. There's only room for those who love him and follow him simply because they love him.

Pope Francis was very clear about the right attitude a Christian should have to follow the Lord. This morning, Monday, May 5, during the Mass celebrated in St. Martha's chapel, he asked us to examine ourselves about the way in which we follow Jesus.

The pope took his cue from the gospel passage from John (6:22-29), which tells the story of the crowd who had been fed by Jesus' miracle of the multiplication of the loaves and fishes. When they couldn't see Jesus anymore they went to look for him "on the other side of the lake." Jesus, he began, "draws the people's attention to some attitudes which are wrong and do harm." After the multiplication of the loaves "the crowd was delighted" with what Jesus had done, so that "they wanted to make him king." But he "withdrew, to be by himself. He went to pray on the mountain. Then these people, who followed him in their hearts, who loved him, discovered that Jesus had gone away and went to look for him. Jesus rebuked them for their behavior: 'Truly, I tell you, you are looking for me, not because you saw signs, but because you ate your fill of the loaves.'" As if to say: "You're looking for me out of self-interest." The pope added, "I believe that it will do us good always to ask ourselves: why do I look for Jesus? Why do I follow Jesus?"

"We're all sinners," explained the Holy Father. So we always have some sort of self-interest, something "that needs to be cleansed in our following of Jesus. We must work on ourselves so that we follow him for his own sake, for love."

But the people about whom the gospel is speaking also loved him. "They really loved him," stressed the pope, because, "he spoke like someone with authority." Nevertheless, there were also advantages. "In my following of Jesus," the bishop of Rome asked again, "am I seeking something that isn't precisely Jesus himself? Are my intentions right or not?" We can get the answer from Jesus' own teachings, which "point to three attitudes which are the wrong way to follow him or to seek God."

The first is vanity, and here the bishop of Rome referred to Jesus' admonitions in Matthew's gospel (6:3-5, 16-17): "When you give alms, do not let your left hand know what your right hand is doing." Again: "But whenever you pray, go into your room and shut the door, and pray to your Father in secret." Last, "Whenever you fast, do not look dismal, like the hypocrites," but "put oil on your head and wash your face," so that your fasting may not be seen by others. Jesus said this, the pope noted, "especially to the leaders who wanted to be seen, because—to call it by its right name—they enjoyed peacocking. They behaved like real peacocks. But Jesus says: no, that won't do! Vanity does no good."

Sometimes "we too do things because we want to be seen," out of vanity. But, the pope warned, vanity is dangerous because it can make us slide toward pride and arrogance. When that happens "it's all over." So, he suggested, we must always ask ourselves: "How do I do things? As for the good things I do, do I do them in secret or in order to be seen?" And if Jesus says that to the leaders, the bosses, it's as if "he were saying so to us, us pastors. A pastor who is vain does the people of God no good." Those leaders about whom Jesus speaks in the gospel loved wearing luxurious clothes, noted the pope, among others things. He confided that when he sees "a pastor, a priest, a bishop going about dressed up to the nines, as if he were going to a worldly reception," he asks himself: "But what do people think of it? That pastor is not following Jesus; be he priest or bishop, he isn't following Jesus. He may follow him a bit but he loves vanity."

That's one of the things Jesus rebuked. In the same way he always rebukes those who pursue power. "Some people followed Jesus because they were unconsciously pursuing power," explained the Holy Father. He recalled the request of James and John, the sons of Zebedee, who wanted a powerful position when the promised kingdom came. "There are social climbers in the church, so many of them . . .," commented the pope. But, he added, it would be better if they "went north for mountaineering and climbed the Alps! It's healthier! Don't come to church to do your climbing!" Jesus, he recalled again, "rebuked those climbers who sought power. He loved James and John very much but when they sought power he told them: you don't know what you're asking for."

The Holy Father reminded us that Jesus' disciples' own desire for power continued up to the last moment, the moment when Jesus was about to ascend into heaven. They thought the kingdom was about to come and they asked the Lord, "Is the kingdom coming now, the moment of our power?" Only when the Holy Spirit comes upon them, he explained, do the disciples understand and change their attitude. But in our Christian lives, "sin remains. And that's why it will do us good to ask ourselves: how do I follow Jesus? For his sake alone and as far as the cross, or do I seek power and use the church, the Christian community, the parish, the diocese to get a bit of power?"

The third thing "that keeps us from having the right intentions is money." Indeed, there are "people who follow Jesus for money and with money," declared the pope without mincing his words. "They try to profit financially from the parish, the diocese, the Christian community, the hospital, the college . . . Think of the first Christian community who endured that temptation, Simon, Ananias and Saphhira . . . So this temptation has been present from the beginning. And we've known so many good Catholics, good Christians, friends, benefactors of the church, even those holding various honors. Then it was discovered that they'd been involved in rather shady dealings. They were really businessmen and they made a lot of money. They presented themselves as benefactors of the church, but they got so much money and that money wasn't always clean."

Here the Holy Father repeated the questions: "How do I follow Jesus? 'Truly, I tell you, you are looking for me, not because you saw signs, but because you ate your fill of the loaves.' In my following of Jesus is there vanity? Is there the desire for power? Is there the desire for money? It will do us good, he urged, to examine our hearts, our consciences, on whether we have the right intentions in following Jesus. Do I follow him for his sake alone? That's the way of holiness. Or do I follow him but also seek some advantage for myself?" That's not Christian. So, he concluded, "let us ask the Lord for the grace to send us the Holy Spirit in order to follow him with the right intentions: for his sake alone, without vanity, without the desire for power, and without the desire for money."

Christian Witness

Tuesday, May 6, 2014
Acts 7:51–8:1a

B earing witness to Christ is the essence of the church, which would otherwise end up being nothing but a sterile "university of religion," proof against the action of the Holy Spirit. Pope Francis reaffirmed this in the Mass celebrated on Tuesday morning, May 6, in the chapel of St. Martha's Guest House.

His meditation on the power of Christian witness was based

on the day's liturgical passage from the Acts of the Apostles (7:51–8:1a), which tells the story of Stephen's martyrdom. The Holy Father explained, it "was a replica of Jesus' martyrdom: the jealousy of the leaders who tried to eliminate him, the false witnesses, the hasty judgment." To his unbelieving persecutors Stephen said: "You stiff-necked and uncircumcised in heart and ears, you are forever opposing the Holy Spirit."

"Those words," commented the pope, "were the very words that Jesus himself had said: 'As your fathers were, so are you; which of the prophets didn't your fathers persecute?'" In fact, Jesus had rebuked them because "they built monuments for the prophets, prophets whom their fathers had killed." So "Stephen, full of the Holy Spirit," says "the same words as Jesus."

Certainly, the Holy Father noted, the persecutors weren't peaceful people with hearts at peace. On the contrary, "these people had hatred in their hearts." The Acts of the Apostles tells us, "When they heard these things they became enraged and ground their teeth at Stephen." So they were people who "felt hatred. They didn't just disagree with what Stephen was preaching; they hated him!" And "that hatred was sown in their hearts by the devil," said the pope. "It's the devil's hatred for Christ."

It is "in martyrdom that we see clearly this struggle between God and the devil," continued Pope Francis. "We see that hatred. It wasn't a peaceful discussion." Besides, he observed, "being persecuted, being martyred, giving your life for Jesus is one of the beatitudes." So Jesus didn't say to his people: 'You poor things! What awful things are happening to you!' No, he said: 'Blessed are you when people revile and persecute you and utter all kinds of evil against you falsely for my sake. Rejoice and be glad!'"

So it's obvious that "the devil can't bear the church's holiness" or "anyone's holiness without reacting," said the pope. "The devil stirred up hatred in those people's hearts to persecute, to revile, to utter all sorts of evil. Thus they killed Stephen," who "dies like Jesus, forgiving." We read in Acts: "Stephen prayed and said, 'Lord Jesus, receive my spirit.'" Yes, the pope repeated, "Stephen said the same as Jesus: 'Lord, do not hold this sin against them.'"

"The Greek word martyrdom means witness," explained the pope. "So we can say that the way for a Christian is to follow in the footsteps of Jesus' own witness in order to bear witness to him." Witness that so often ends with sacrificing your life: "Being a Christian has got to mean bearing witness, being a witness."

The central point, declared the pope, is that Christianity is not a religion "just about ideas, theology, aesthetics, commandments. We are a people who follow Jesus Christ and bear witness, who want to bear witness to Jesus Christ. And that witness sometimes leads to giving your life."

The story of Stephen's martyrdom is eloquent. The passage from Acts continues: "That day a severe persecution began against the church in Jerusalem." So "with Stephen's death, persecution broke out against them all." The persecutors "felt strong; the devil stirred them to unleash that violent persecution."

The persecution was so brutal that "with the exception of the apostles who remained there, in place, the Christians were scattered throughout the region of Judea and Samaria." It was "persecution that drove the Christians to go far away." Then when they met people "they told them why" they were fleeing; "they explained the gospel, they bore witness to Jesus. Thus the church's mission began. Many were converted when they heard what these people were saying."

The bishop of Rome recalled that "one of the fathers of the church said, the blood of martyrs is the seed of Christians." That's just what happened. "Persecution broke out, the Christians were scattered, and they preached the faith by their witness." For, the pope noted, "witness is always fruitful" when it occurs in daily life, but also when it occurs in difficult times or when it even leads to death.

So the church "is a fruitful mother when she bears witness to Jesus Christ. But when the church closes in on herself, when she thinks of herself—let's put it this way—as a university of religion with so many fine ideas, so many fine buildings, fine museums, so many fine things but doesn't bear witness, she becomes barren."

The same goes for individual Christians, added the pope. If "they don't bear witness they are barren; they don't give the life they have received from Jesus Christ."

The Acts of the Apostles tells us "that Stephen was full of the Holy Spirit." Indeed, "we can't bear witness without the presence of the Holy Spirit in us. There are difficult times when we have to choose the right path, when we have to say no to so many things that may be trying to seduce us. These are times that call for prayer to the Holy Spirit. It's he who makes us strong to go the way of witness."

In conclusion, Pope Francis recalled how "the two images" offered by the liturgy—Stephen who dies and the Christians who bear witness far and wide—give rise to certain questions for each one of us: "What sort of witness do I bear? Am I a Christian witness to Jesus or simply a member of a sect? Am I fruitful in bearing witness or do I remain barren because I'm not capable of letting the Holy Spirit carry me forward in my Christian vocation?"

No Bureaucracy in the Sacristy

Thursday, May 8, 2014
Acts 8:26-40

Sometimes there are negative attitudes which make it difficult to hear the Lord's call and difficult to talk with someone else in a way that pays real attention to who that person is and real-

izes the power of grace. These are the three fundamental requirements for preaching the gospel. Negative attitudes, which in the
church take the shape of "bureaucracy" that makes it its "business
to create impediments to keep people from the sacraments."

The pope issued a call to become "facilitators of the sacraments" during the Mass celebrated on Thursday morning, May
8, in the chapel of St. Martha's Guest House.

The passage from the Acts of the Apostles (8:26-40) in the
day's liturgy presents these three requirements clearly, said the
pope. "The first one," he explained, "is Philip's readiness when
he goes to proclaim Jesus Christ." He is involved "in his work
of preaching the gospel," when "the angel of the Lord tells
him: get up, leave this and go that way, along that road." Philip
obeys; "he's ready to hear to the Lord's call" and goes where
the Lord tells him. "That shows us that without this readiness
to hear God's voice no one can preach the gospel, no one can
proclaim Jesus Christ. By and large, you will just be proclaiming yourself."

"The second requirement for preaching the gospel is conversation," continued the pope. The Acts of the Apostles tells us that
on the road Philip meets "an Ethiopian eunuch, a court official
of the Candace, queen of the Ethiopians," a region where women
governed, noted the pope, also citing the "queen of Sheba." That
man was "in charge of the entire treasury," of her kingdom, a
real "treasury minister." He had come "to Jerusalem to worship,
because he was a Jew." Acts tells us that the minister was "seated
in his chariot, reading the prophet Isaiah." Then the Lord said to
Philip, "Go ahead and approach that chariot." Hearing that the
man "was reading the prophet," Philip "took courage and asked
him: 'Do you understand what you are reading?'" This is the very
point which leads us to "the second requirement in the process
of preaching the gospel: conversation." But having a conversation doesn't just mean saying only "what I think" and expecting

the other person to believe me, said the pope. On the contrary, a proper conversation "starts with the other person: do you understand what you are reading?"

Thus preaching the gospel takes its cue for conversation from the other person, "it humbles itself before the other person. It doesn't impose ideas, doctrines," saying, "that's how things are!" True preaching of the gospel goes out to meet the other person, "to offer Jesus' salvation" and "does so humbly through conversation." It is aware that "you can't preach the gospel without conversation," and you can't ignore the position of the other person "to whom you are trying to preach." The pope then raised a possible objection: "But, Father, this wastes such a lot of time, because everyone has their own story, their own ideas . . ." That's true, he recognized. Doing it this way "means spending time" but "God surely spent a lot more time creating the world! And he did it well!" So it's necessary "to spend time with the other person, because that person is the one to whom God wants you to preach the gospel," to whom you must give "news of Jesus." It's also important that the conversation should be with the person "as they are now" and "not as they ought to be."

Turning back to the story in the Acts of the Apostles, the pope pointed out that the conversation between Philip and the minister must have been a long one and focused on baptism, because "when they came to a place where there was water the eunuch said: 'Look, here is water! What is to prevent me from being baptized?'"

That brings us to the third requirement for preaching the gospel, said the pope. "That man had felt the power of God within himself" and when he sees water he asks the apostle, what is to prevent me from being baptized? And Philip said nothing but made him get down from the chariot and "baptized him in the water." Here we see "the power of the sacrament, the power of grace," said the pope. Thus the process of preaching the gospel is completed: readiness of the one preaching, conversation with the other person, and the power of grace. "Philip takes this man of good will, a good man, and brings him into God's hands, God's grace."

This "third requirement" for preaching the gospel suggested a reflection to Pope Francis "on the question the treasury minister asks: Look, here's water! What is to prevent me from being baptized? What is to prevent grace from coming to me?"

"So often," the pope reflected, "we distance people from an encounter with God, we distance them from grace," because we don't behave as "facilitators of the sacraments."

The story in the Acts of the Apostles continues and shows us the end of the preaching process. For "when they came up out of the water, the Spirit of the Lord snatched Philip away and the eunuch saw him no more." That's the confirmation that God was present in this process of preaching the gospel. On the one hand, the bishop of Rome explained, "the eunuch went on his way rejoicing"; on the other, "Philip found himself at Azotus, where he proclaimed the gospel to the people." Here's the moral: that man who came from far away wasn't very learned, but was reading the Bible because he had been taught in the synagogue. But he had goodwill and then he felt the joy of grace, grace which "is gratis, which can't be bought because it isn't for sale: it is given." And "with this joy that man, who couldn't have children because he was a eunuch, carried within him the seed of life to his people and produced a Christian people." Later Matthew and Mark also went to that region "to found churches."

The passage from Acts, remarked the pope, "will help us to realize that the one preaching the gospel is God: 'No one can come to me unless the Father who sent me draws him.' It's the Father who draws us to Jesus." And, he added, "Jesus had said to Philip on another occasion, 'Philip, the Father and I are one.'"

In conclusion, the pope invited us to think about "those three requirements for preaching the gospel: readiness of the one preaching" to do God's will, "conversation with other people" just as they are, and "trusting in grace," because "grace is more important than any bureaucracy." He invited us to reflect well on the eunuch's question: "What is to prevent me from being baptized?" Finally, the pope noted: "So often we in the church become a business creating impediments to keep people from coming to grace. May the Lord make us understand that."

Who Decreases and Who Increases

Friday, May 9, 2014
Acts 9:1-20; John 6:52-59

The witness of St. John Paul II, like that of "so many great saints" in the church's history, shows us that the rule of holiness is "to decrease so that the Lord may increase." And "we all saw the final days of St. John Paul II: he couldn't speak. God's great athlete, God's great warrior, ended up like that. He was wiped out by illness. Humiliated like Jesus." Recalling the witness of Pope Wojtyla—canonized on April 27, 2014, together with John XXIII—the pope described the profile of holiness in his homily at the Mass celebrated on Friday morning, May 9, in the chapel of St. Martha's Guest House. The saints, he said, aren't heroes but women and men who live with the cross in their daily lives: they are people chosen by God to show that the church is holy, even though she is composed of sinners.

"The church is holy." That was the truth inspiring Pope Francis' homily. He began with a question: how can the church be holy if all of us who are in it are sinners? Actually, he said, "we are sinners but the church is holy; she's the bride of Jesus Christ and he loves her, he makes her holy. He makes her holy every day by his Eucharistic sacrifice because he loves her so much." So "we are sinners but in a holy church."

"By belonging to the church we too are made holy: we are the church's children and Mother Church makes us holy by her love, by the sacraments of her bridegroom." In practice, continued the bishop of Rome, "this is everyday holiness, this is the holiness of us all. So when the Acts of the Apostles speaks of Christians they are called 'the saints.'" St. Paul also "speaks to the saints: to us, who are sinners but children of holy church, made holy through the body and blood of Jesus, as we heard just now in the gospel" of John (6:52-59).

In this holy church, declared Pope Francis, "the Lord chooses some people to show its holiness better, to show that it's he who sanctifies; that no one can sanctify themselves of their own accord; that there is no set course to becoming a saint; that being a saint doesn't mean behaving like a fakir" or something. Rather, "holiness is a gift from Jesus to his church; and to show this he chooses some people," in whom "his sanctifying work can be clearly seen."

Today's liturgy shows us "the sanctification of Saul, Paul," related in the Acts of the Apostles (9:1-20). He is not an isolated case because in the gospel there are so many figures of holiness. For example, continued the pope, "there's Mary Magdalene. In his gospel St. Mark tells us that Jesus had cast seven devils out of her" and thus "he makes her holy: from being the worst to being a saint!" Then "there's Matthew, who was a traitor to his people and took money from them to give to the Romans." But "the Lord takes him from his business" and takes him along with himself. Then "there's Zacchaeus who wants to see Jesus. And Jesus calls him—'come, come with me'—and makes him holy."

"But why in the church's history does the Lord choose these

people?" asked the pope, recalling that over the two thousand years of Christianity "there have been so many saints who have been recognized as saints by the church." The Lord chooses these people, was his reply, so that they may bear clearer witness to the first law of holiness: Christ must increase and we must decrease. What occurs is "our humbling so that the Lord may increase."

That's why the Lord "chooses Saul, an enemy of the church," as the Acts of the Apostles tells us. Saul, still breathing threats and murder against the disciples of the Lord, "went to the high priest and asked him for letters to the synagogues at Damascus, so that if he found any who belonged to the Way, men or women, he might bring them bound to Jerusalem."

Strong words which show how much Saul hated and persecuted the church, a hatred, noted the bishop of Rome, which "we also saw in the stoning of Stephen." Saul was present at it too. Filled with that hatred, he "goes to ask for permission" to persecute the Christians. "But the Lord awaits him; he awaits him and makes him feel his power," said the pope. Then Saul "is struck blind and obeys" when the Lord says to him on the road to Damascus: "Get up and enter the city and you will be told what you are to do."

Thus "from being a man who had everything clear, who knew what had to be done against this sect of Christians, he becomes like a child and obeys: he gets up and goes to wait." But Saul "doesn't wait with a mobile in his hand," saying, "Come on . . . what must I do . . . tell me . . . I've been waiting for two days . . ." Instead, "he waits just as he is: praying and fasting. His heart is changed."

The story in Acts then introduces Ananias, who baptizes Paul. So finally, "Paul gets up, eats some food, and then goes off to the synagogues proclaiming that Jesus is the Son of God." He starts "a different life."

At this point the pope remarked on the difference between

heroes and saints, repeating the words that the Lord says to Ananias: "Go, for he is an instrument whom I have chosen to bring my name before the Gentiles and kings, and before the people of Israel. I myself will show him how much he must suffer for the sake of my name."

So, explained the pope, "the difference between heroes and saints is witness, the imitation of Jesus Christ: going the way of Jesus Christ." Therefore, "Paul preaches the gospel, is persecuted, flogged, condemned, and ends his life with a small group of friends in Rome, in the hands of his disciples." Thus Paul "decreases, decreases, decreases," in accordance with the rule of holiness. The pope then mentioned again the figure of John the Baptist, "the greatest man born of woman, who ends up in prison at the whim of a dancer and through the hatred of an adulteress."

So "Paul ends up in the common way. Surely one morning three, four, or five soldiers came for him" and ordered him: "Come with us!" Then "they took him away and cut off his head. Just like that." Paul, "the great man who had traveled the world, ends up like that." That, repeated the pope, "is the difference between a hero and a saint: the saint is someone who follows Jesus, follows the way of Jesus, the way of the cross."

"So many saints canonized by the church," declared the pope, "ended up so humbly." They are "the great saints." Then Pope Francis returned to the witness of St. John Paul II. "That's the way to holiness for the great saints." But it's "also the way to holiness for us." Because, he explained, of course "we won't be saints if we don't allow our hearts to be changed along this way of Jesus: carrying the cross every day, the ordinary cross, the simple cross and letting Jesus increase. If we don't go that way we won't be saints, but if we do, we shall bear witness to Jesus Christ, who loves us so much. We shall bear witness that whereas we are sinners, the church is holy, she's the bride of Christ."

So "today," the pope concluded, "perhaps it will do us good during Mass to feel the joy of knowing that Jesus' sacrifice here on the altar sanctifies us all, makes us grow in holiness, makes us become more genuinely children of his bride, the church our mother who is holy."

We Are All Doorkeepers

Monday, May 12, 2014
Acts 11:1-18

In the church we are all, without exception, charged with exercising the ancient ministry of doorkeeper or porter, that is, "the one who opens the doors" and "welcomes people." Moreover, in the whole history of the church there has never been an office of "the one who shuts the doors" in people's faces.

So the pope issued an invitation not to "cage" the Holy Spirit at the Mass celebrated on Monday morning, May 12, in the chapel of St. Martha's Guest House. In his homily the bishop of Rome began with a page from the Acts of the Apostles (11:1-18), which, he confided, he regards "as one of its finest passages," that "has such a lot to teach us bishops." It begins strongly, he said: "Now the apostles and the brothers who were in Judea heard that the Gentiles had also accepted the word of God. So when Peter went up to Jerusalem, the circumcised brothers criticized him, saying, 'You went into uncircumcised men's houses and ate with them!'"

In their eyes "this was scandalous," something they had "never thought" could happen. Indeed, for them it was unimaginable to go into a house and even sit at table with the uncircumcised, because that was unclean. Peter had not only done so but even baptized those people. In short, said the pope, they regarded him as a "madman." Just as if "tomorrow an expedition arrived of little green men from Mars with long noses and big ears, as they are depicted by children." But if one of these Martians said, "I want to be baptized," what would happen?

So according to the Acts of the Apostles, Peter "tells them what had happened, how it had been the Spirit" who drove him to it. It was "the same Spirit who had told Philip to go and baptize that treasury minister of the Candace," as we also read in Acts.

It was the Spirit "who drove Peter to go" on, encouraged him, because "nothing is unclean." And Peter obeyed. Then, the pope recalled, "we know what happened: the baptism of Cornelius and his whole household." Peter responds to the rebukes "from the brothers belonging to the church of Jerusalem by saying, 'If God gave them the same gift that he gave us when we believed in the Lord Jesus Christ, who was I to hinder God?'"

A question which applies to each of us today, declared the pope, because "when the Lord shows us the way, who are we to say, No, Lord, that's unwise, no, let's do this?" It was Peter "who made the decision" and said, "Who am I to hinder?" That's a really "beautiful thing to say," explained the pope, "for bishops, priests, and also for lay people. Who are we to shut the doors?" It's not accidental that in the church there has always been a "doorkeeper," who is the one who opens the door, welcomes people, and lets them in, but there has "never been an office of one who shuts the door, never!"

Besides, continued the pope, the Lord told the disciples he would send "another Advocate," who, he promised, "will guide you into all truth." So "the Lord leaves the guidance of his church to the Holy Spirit." That also goes for today, because "the Lord has left the guidance of the church in the hands of the Holy Spirit. It is he who guides us all with the grace we have received at baptism and in the sacraments."

The Holy Spirit's mission didn't end on the day of Pentecost when he came down upon them and then there was "such an uproar" that "people were saying perhaps these folk didn't have coffee for breakfast but a good slug of wine!" Actually, "they weren't drunk." The story "began" on that day and from then on "the Spirit has been carrying on, leading the church forward."

For, the pope noted, the behavior of "the Jerusalem Christians who were good believers" is "interesting." After having rebuked Peter and called him a "madman," they listened to his explanation. Then "they calmed down and began to praise God saying, 'Then God has given even to the Gentiles the repentance that leads to life!'"

So it's "the Holy Spirit who, as Jesus said, will teach us everything." He will make us "remember what Jesus taught us." The Spirit "is God's living presence in the church; he's the one that keeps the church going, who enables the church always to carry on, beyond the limits, go further." He's the one "who guides the church with his gifts. It's impossible to think of Jesus' church without that Advocate whom the Lord sends us" and who leads us "to those unthinkable choices." To use John XXIII's word: it's the Holy Spirit who brings the church up to date (*aggiornamento*) and enables her to carry on.

Then the pope invited Christians "to ask the Lord for the grace to be receptive to the Holy Spirit, receptive to that Spirit who speaks to us in our hearts, who speaks to us in life's situations, who speaks to us in our church life, in the Christian community, who always tells us: go ahead, make decisions, do that . . ." The pope also suggested that we should always remember Peter's question: Who am I to hinder the Holy Spirit? Who am I to change the office of doorkeeper in the church and say, this far and no further? Who am I to cage the Holy Spirit?

In answering these questions, the bishop of Rome prayed

"that the Lord may give us the calm that befell those Christians in Judea" after they had listened to Peter, "and may he also give us the grace to praise God." Those Jewish Christians said, "Then God has given even to the Gentiles repentance that leads to life." Pope Francis concluded, today we also say this to those people so far from the church who may have a negative opinion of her, "God grant that they may be converted and have life, because the Holy Spirit rules supreme."

Those Who Open Doors

Tuesday, May 13, 2014
Acts 11:19-26; John 10:22-30

The Holy Spirit is always active. It's up to Christians to welcome him or not. But there's a difference, which can be seen plainly: Those who are receptive and welcome him live in joy and openness to others. But those who shut themselves off, because they consider themselves "an intellectual aristocracy," claiming to understand the things of God with their heads alone, become separated from the reality of the church. To the point where they no longer believe, even when there is a miracle. Pope Francis introduced these two opposite attitudes during the Mass celebrated on Tuesday morning, May 13, in the chapel of St. Martha's Guest House.

The day's liturgical readings (Acts of the Apostles 11:19-26 and John 10:22-30), explained the bishop of Rome, "present a diptych: two groups of people." In the passage from Acts we meet first of all those "who had been scattered because persecution had broken out" after Stephen's martyrdom. "They were scattered" but "everywhere they brought with them the seed of the gospel," at first only to the Jews. "Then quite naturally," the pope continued, "some of them, people from Cyprus and Cyrene who came to Antioch, began also to speak to the Hellenists, proclaiming that Jesus was Lord." Thus "slowly they opened the doors to the Greeks, the Gentiles."

When this news reached the Jerusalem church, they sent Barnabas to Antioch "on an inspection visit," to check what was happening in person. The book of Acts relates that "they were all happy" and that "a great many people were brought to the Lord."

In short, declared the pope, in order to preach the gospel "these people didn't say: let's go first to the Jews, then to the Hellenists, then to the Gentiles, then to everybody." But "they let themselves be led by the Holy Spirit: they were amenable to the Holy Spirit." In this way "one thing followed another" and then "another and yet another still," and they "ended up opening the doors to everybody." Even "to the Gentiles," the pope pointed out, "who to their minds were unclean." Those Christians "opened the doors to everybody" without making any distinctions.

That, explained the pope, "is the first group of people" presented in today's liturgy. They consisted of people "amenable to the Holy Spirit," who "go ahead as Paul did" just "naturally." For, he noted, "sometimes the Holy Spirit drives us to do bold things, as he drove Philip to go and baptize that gentleman from Ethiopia" and "as he drove Peter to go and baptize Cornelius." On other occasions "the Spirit leads us gently." So true virtue means "letting ourselves be led by the Holy Spirit: not resisting the Holy Spirit, being amenable to the Holy Spirit." And being certain that "the Holy Spirit is active today in the church, active in our own lives today." Maybe, the pope continued, "one of you might say, but I've never seen him! So pay attention to what happens, what comes into your mind, what comes into your heart: good things; it's the Holy Spirit inviting you to go that way." But of course, "you need to be receptive to the Holy Spirit."

So now we come to the second group of people in the "diptych" presented to us by the liturgy. A group, the bishop of Rome explained, made up of "intellectuals, who approach Jesus in the temple: the doctors of the law." These were men who always had "a problem because they never came to understand; they were always circling round things, because they believed religion was only headwork, a matter of law, creating with commandments, keeping commandments and nothing else." These people, the pope continued, "didn't even imagine the Holy Spirit existed." So—we read in John's gospel—"they approached and gathered round Jesus saying: 'How long will you keep us in suspense? If you are the Christ, tell us plainly!'" To which "Jesus answered simply, 'I have told you and you do not believe. The works I do in my Father's name testify to me.'" As if to say, "Look at the people miraculously cured, look at the things I do, listen to the words I say!" But those men only looked "to what they had in their heads." So "they went round and round with arguments, they wanted to go on and on discussing." Indeed for them "everything was headwork, everything was intellectual."

The thing was, said the pope, that "in those people there was no heart, no love of beauty, no harmony. They were people who only wanted explanations." But even if "you give them explanations, they immediately come back, unconvinced, with another question." In this way "they go round and round, as they circled round Jesus all his life, until the moment when they managed to catch him and kill him." These, continued the pope, are people who "don't open their hearts to the Holy Spirt" and who "believe that the things of God can only be understood with the head, by ideas, their own ideas: they are proud, they believe they know everything and anything that doesn't enter their minds isn't true."

If you were to "raise someone from the dead before them, they wouldn't believe!"

In the gospel we see that "Jesus goes further and says something very forceful: why don't you believe? You don't believe because you don't belong to my flock! You don't believe because you don't belong to the people of Israel, you've left them!" And he continues: "You think yourselves so pure and you can't believe like that!" The Lord points clearly to their attitude which "closes up the heart," and so "they have rejected the people." Jesus says to them: "You are like your fathers who killed the prophets!" Because "when a prophet came who said something they didn't like they killed him!"

The real problem, noted the pope, is that "they had detached themselves from the people of God and so they couldn't believe." In fact, "faith is a gift of God, but faith comes if you belong to his people; or if you are now in the church; if you are helped by the sacraments, by your brothers and sisters, by the congregation: if you believe that this church is the people of God." Whereas "those folk had detached themselves, they didn't believe in the people of God; they only believed in their own ideas and thus they had built up a whole system of commandments, which drove people away and didn't allow them into the church, to become one of God's people." With that attitude "they couldn't believe" and that's the sin of "resisting the Holy Spirit."

So, repeated the pope, here we have "two groups." On the one hand, we have "the kind, humble ones who are amenable to the Holy Spirit." But on the other, we have "the proud, self-sufficient, arrogant ones, detached from the people, intellectual aristocrats, who have shut the doors and resist the Holy Spirit." They are not "just stubborn, but something worse: they have hard hearts." That's even "more dangerous." Jesus warns them by saying explicitly: "You are hard of heart"; and he "also says so to the disciples on the road to Emmaus."

By "looking at these two groups," concluded Pope Francis, "let us ask the Lord for the grace of being amenable to the Holy Spirit to carry on in life, be creative, be joyful." The hard-hearted aren't joyful; they're always grim. The pope warned, "when there's so much grimness the Spirt of God isn't there." So "let us ask the Lord for the grace of receptivity and that the Holy Spirit may help us defend ourselves against that other wrong spirit of self-sufficiency, pride, arrogance, with hearts closed to the Holy Spirit."

Memory and Hope

Thursday, May 15, 2014
Acts 13:13-25

Jesus isn't a lone hero who came down from heaven to save us; he's the focal point and final end of the story God began with his people. So a Christian must always be Eucharistic, proceeding with memory and hope, never a solitary unit. For if we don't journey with people, if we don't belong to the church, faith is something artificial, cooked up in the laboratory. This is what Pope Francis said during the Mass celebrated on Thursday, May 15, in the chapel of St. Martha's Guest House.

"It's curious," noted the pope, "that when the apostles proclaim Jesus Christ they never begin with Jesus himself," his person, "saying: Jesus Christ is the savior!" No, the apostles always begin their testimony by starting from the "history of the people." We see that today, he pointed out, in the passage from the Acts of the Apostles (13:13-25), which gives us the testimony of St. Paul at Antioch in Pisidia. "But Peter does the same in his first speeches and Stephen had also done the same."

Thus, when the apostles are asked, "why do you believe in this man?" they start talking about "Abraham and the whole history of the people." The reason for this is clear: "Jesus can't be understood without that history; Jesus is the end point of that story, he is where the story leads, where it is going."

So, we read in the Acts of the Apostles that Paul stood up in the synagogue and said, "Men of Israel, the God of this people Israel chose our fathers." Paul says "chose our fathers," beginning his speech "with God's choosing one man, Abraham," whom he commanded to leave his country and the home of his fathers. God chose him, explained the pope, thereby beginning "a journey for which they have been chosen. The people of God is a chosen people, but they're always on a journey."

That's why, declared the pope, "Jesus Christ can't be understood without this history of preparation for him." Consequently, "a Christian makes no sense outside the people of God." Because "a Christian is not a lone, single unit. No, he or she belongs to a people, the church." To the point where "a Christian without the church is purely a figment, unreal!"

For, he continued, we have "God's promise": I will make you a great people! So "this people journeys with a promise!" Here the dimension of memory comes in: "It's important that in our lives we keep the dimension of memory present," stressed the pope. In fact, he added, "Christians are 'mindful' of the history of their people; 'mindful' of their church." So Christians are people who bear in mind, who keep "the memory" of the past.

In that dimension of memory "the people journey toward the final promise, toward fulfillment; they're a chosen people who have a promise for the future and journey toward that promise, toward the fulfillment of that promise." So, he explained, "a Christian in the church is a man or a woman with hope. Hope in the promise, hope which isn't expectation but something else! It's hope, so go ahead! It's hope that doesn't disappoint!" Thus, "looking back, Christians are 'mindful'; they always ask for the grace of memory!" And "looking forward, a Christian is a man or a woman with hope." Between memory and hope "Christians in the present pursue God's way and renew the covenant with God." In practice, "they continually say to the Lord, yes, I want the commandments, I want your will, I want to follow you!" By doing so they become "covenant people." For, said the pope, "we celebrate the covenant here every day," on the altar. So a Christian is always "a Eucharistic woman or man."

In that context, the bishop of Rome made clear, "a Christian can't be understood as a lone single unit," just as "Jesus can't be understood on his own." In fact, "Jesus Christ didn't fall from heaven like a hero coming to save us. No, Jesus Christ has a history!" And "we may say—and this is true—that God has a history because he wanted to journey with us." That's why "Jesus Christ can't be understood without his history." That's also why "a Christian without a history, a Christian without a people, a Christian without the church makes no sense: it's something cooked up in a laboratory, something artificial, something that can have no life."

Then Pope Francis' meditation led to an examination of conscience: what is our Christian identity like? Let us ask ourselves, he suggested, "whether our Christian identity means belonging to a people, the church." Because if it isn't, "we're not Christians." But "we came into the church by baptism."

So it's important, the pope said again, "to get into the habit of asking for the grace of memory of the journey made by the people of God." Also for the grace of "personal memory: what has God done with me in my life, how has he made me keep going?" He then continued, we should also "ask for the grace of hope, which isn't optimism; it's something else." Finally, "ask for the grace to renew every day the covenant with the Lord by which we have been summoned." The pope concluded: "May the Lord give us these three graces which are necessary to Christian identity."

Three Doors

Friday, May 16, 2015
Acts 13:26-33; John 14:1-6

Praying, celebrating, imitating Jesus are the three "doors" to open in order to find "the way to the truth and the life." That's what Pope Francis said this morning, Friday, May 16, during the Mass in the chapel of St. Martha's Guest House. In fact, according to the pope, Jesus can't be reached purely by theoretical study and anyone trying to do so risks sliding into heresy. On the contrary, we must continually ask ourselves how prayer, celebration, and the imitation of Christ come into our lives. "Let's think about these three doors and it will do all of us good," he said. He suggested we start by reading the book of the gospel, which too often grows dusty, because it's never opened. Pick it up, open it, he urged, and you will find Jesus.

After reminding us that his reflection on the previous day had been focused on the fact that "Christian life is always a journey along a road and not alone," but always "in the church, among the people of God," the bishop of Rome noted that in the liturgical readings for today—taken from the Acts of the Apostles (13:26-33) and John's gospel (14:1-6)—Jesus himself tells us "that he is the way: I am the way, the truth, and the life. Everything. I give you life, I manifest myself as truth, and if you come with me, I am the way." This means that in order to know the one who calls himself "the way, the truth, and the life," we have to set out "on a journey." Thus, according to Pope Francis, "knowing Jesus is the most important work of our lives." That's also because by knowing him we come to know the Father.

But, asked the pope, "how can we know Jesus?" The pope agreed with those who answer, "We must study a lot," and he invited us "to study the catechism: a beautiful book, the *Catechism of the Catholic Church,* and we should study it." But, he added at once, we shouldn't limit ourselves "to thinking that we can know Jesus just by studying." Actually, some people "imagine that ideas and ideas alone will lead us to the knowledge of Jesus." "Among the early Christians" too, some people thought that way "and they ended up rather muddled in their thinking." For "ideas on their own don't give life" and so anyone going that way "ends up in a labyrinth," from which "they can't get out." For that very reason, from the beginning in the church, "there have been heresies," which are "trying to understand who Jesus is with our minds alone." The pope recalled the words of "a great English writer," Gilbert Keith Chesterton, who defined heresy as an idea gone mad. Indeed, said the pope, "that's it: ideas on their own go mad."

So he pointed to the three doors to open in order to "know Jesus." Beginning with the first door—prayer—the pope repeated that "study without prayer doesn't work. The great theologians do theology on their knees." For although "by study we come a bit closer, without prayer we will never know Jesus."

As for the second door—celebrating—the bishop of Rome declared that even prayer on its own "isn't enough: we also need the joy of celebrating, celebrating Jesus in his sacraments, because it's there he gives us life, gives us strength, gives us food, gives us comfort, gives us the covenant, gives us a mission. Without the celebration of the sacraments we don't come to know Jesus. The sacraments belong to the church."

Finally, to open the third door, the *imitatio Christi,* the task is to take up the gospel in order to discover "what he did, what his life was like, what he said to us, what he taught us," so that we can "try to imitate him." In conclusion, the pope explained that going through these three doors means "entering into the mystery of Jesus." In fact, we "can only know him if we are capable of entering into his mystery." And we shouldn't be afraid of doing so.

So at the end of his homily Pope Francis invited us to think "during the day about what's happening with the door of prayer in my life, prayer of the heart," true prayer.

On the Move and Steadfast

Monday, May 19, 2014
ACTS 14:5-18; JOHN 14:21-26

On the move and steadfast. During the Mass celebrated at St. Martha's on Monday morning, May 19, these were the two attitudes suggested to Christians by Pope Francis so as not to let ourselves be overwhelmed by the events and difficulties we have to face every day.

Referring to the reading from the Acts of the Apostles (14:5-18), the bishop of Rome turned back to the story of the Gentiles and Jews attempting to stone Paul and Barnabas at Iconium. So they both fled to take refuge in Lystra and Derbe, cities of Lycaonia, and the surrounding country. In particular, Paul "flees," explained the pope, "and begins preaching the gospel," showing "his capacity always to keep beginning all over again, not giving way to moaning." His heart is set on what he knows is his mission, preaching the gospel. His is the right attitude for a Christian. The pope recalled that the Collect that had just been read prayed the Lord to grant us that "amid the changes and chances of the world our hearts might be set where true joy is to be found." He pointed out two requirements for Christian life: "being on the move and steadfast. A heart set, a heart fixed, but in continual movement. We see this clearly in Paul's work of preaching the gospel."

Still referring to the Acts, the pope recalled the episode of Paul's meeting with the paralyzed man. "With his steadfast heart," explained the pope, "he was able to understand that paralyzed man lying there had the faith to be healed. He was able to discern it and he healed him in the Lord's name." But Paul certainly didn't expect the reaction of the people who had been present at the healing. Actually, there was a little "revolution," because they all believed that "Barnabas was Zeus and Paul was Hermes. Paul strove to convince them that they were just human men."

Here, the bishop of Rome noted, "we move on to another state of mind, struggle," because the people even wanted to honor them by a sacrifice. Paul struggles "to explain to them that there is only one God." In order to do so, "he doesn't speak here directly about Jesus," but speaks their own language "about God the Creator," showing that he knows the right way to speak to those he's addressing.

"These are the human events Paul had to cope with," said the pope. "We too have to cope with so many things ourselves. We live among so many changes and chances that we move from one thing to another, but we ask for the grace to have our hearts set, as Paul did, not complaining about persecution, but going to another city to begin preaching there, healing a sick man, realizing that this man had enough faith to be cured. Then he calmed down those enthusiastic people who wanted to offer them a sacrifice. Then he proclaimed that there is only one God in the language of their own culture."

Paul does one thing after another, without stopping. That, the pope noted, "can only come from a heart that is set" on the mission of preaching the gospel, a heart that is able "to make so many changes in such a short time," facing up to situations "adequately."

"In the gospel," continued the pope, referring to the passage from John (14:21-26), "Jesus tells us something: 'I have said these things to you while I am still with you. But the Advocate, the

Holy Spirit, whom the Father will send in my name, will teach you everything and remind you of all that I have said to you.'" So our hearts must be "set on the Holy Spirit," a gift "that Jesus has sent us. Paul had his heart set on the Holy Spirit, and if we want to find steadfastness in our lives amid the human changes and chances we all go through, all of us must do the same. The Holy Spirit is in our hearts, we received him in baptism. The Holy Spirit gives us strength, gives us steadfastness to go forward in life amid so many ups and downs."

For, said Pope Francis, "Jesus tells us two things about this Holy Spirit: he will teach you everything and remind you of everything. We saw how he showed Paul what he should do when Paul moved on to somewhere else." The Holy Spirit teaches and reminds us.

But "what does the Holy Spirit remind Paul of?" asked the pope. First of all "he reminds him of the message of salvation: God wants to save you. Paul's central focus is this: God wants to save us in Jesus Christ. So it was the Holy Spirit who made Paul's heart steadfast. Amid persecutions, problems, discussions, envy, jealousy." In this chapter of the Acts of the Apostles there is "a word that's repeated: jealousy. The jealousy of the leaders of the synagogue," who opposed Paul. But he still manages to go ahead and overcome "so many problems, because his heart is set on the Holy Spirit."

According to the pope, this episode should lead Christians to ask ourselves: "How's my heart? Is it a heart like a ballet dancer who hops about all over the place, or like a butterfly who flits hither one minute then thither, at will? Is it a heart afraid of the changes and chances of life, that hides away and is frightened of bearing witness to Jesus Christ? Is it a brave heart or is it a heart so timid that it always tries to hide? What does our heart care for? What is the treasure on which our heart is set? Is it a heart set on creatures, on the problems we all have? Is it a heart set on our everyday gods or a heart set on the Holy Spirit? Where is the steadfastness of our heart?"

"It will do us good," he added, "to ask ourselves these things. Also to remember all the things going on in our lives every day: at home, at work, with our children, with the people who live with us, with our work colleagues, with everybody." Then the bishop of Rome asked, do we let ourselves be overwhelmed by any of "these things" or do we face them "with a heart set where the only one who can make them steadfast is to be found, the Holy Spirit?" Certainly, he concluded, "it will do us good to think that we have a beautiful gift, left to us by Jesus: that Spirit of steadfastness, of counsel, which helps us carry on. Carry on amid the changes and chances of everyday life. Let us do this exercise today of asking how our heart is. Is it steadfast or not? And if it's steadfast, what is it set on? Is it set on things or on the Holy Spirit?"

Like a Child with a Present

Tuesday, May 20, 2014
John 14:27-31

True peace is a person: the Holy Spirit. "It's a gift of God" to be welcomed and kept as "a child does when given a present." But pay attention to the different kinds of "peace" which the world offers: the false security of money, power, or vanity. These are only illusory kinds of peace and not secure. Pope Francis suggested some practical advice for living in true peace at the Mass celebrated on Tuesday, May 20, in the chapel of St. Martha's Guest House.

The starting point of his meditation was some words from Jesus' farewell speech to his disciples, as they are reported in John's gospel (14:27-31): "Peace I leave with you: my peace I give to you." So peace "is a gift he gives just before going away," explaining: "I do not give it to you as the world gives. Do not let your hearts be troubled, and do not let them be afraid."

So, declared the pope, "the Lord gives us peace: it's a gift he gives before going to his passion." But Jesus tells them: "my peace is not the peace the world gives." It is "a different peace." What, asked the bishop of Rome, is "the peace the world gives us?"

The pope answered this question by describing three aspects of it. The peace the world gives, he began, "is a bit superficial," it's "peace that doesn't reach the depths of the soul." So it's peace that offers "a certain tranquility and a certain joy," but only "up to a point."

One kind of peace the world offers, for example, is "the peace of wealth," which leads us to think: "But I'm at peace because I've got everything organized, I've got enough to live on for the rest of my life, I don't have to worry!" That idea of peace rests on the conviction: "Don't worry, you won't have any problems because you have so much money!" But Jesus himself reminds us "not to trust that peace because, he tells us with great realism, Look out, there are thieves! And thieves can rob you of your money!" So that's why "the peace that money brings is not lasting."

Besides, added the pope, let's not forget "that metal turns rusty." All you need is "a fall in the stock market and all your money is gone," he said in order to stress again that the peace money brings "isn't secure" but only "a superficial, temporary peace." In order to make us understand that better, Jesus tells the story of the vanishing peace of that man "whose barns were full of corn" and he was planning to fill more barns on the next day so that then he could rest "calmly, in peace." But the Lord said to him: "You fool, tonight you will die!" So you see the peace of wealth "doesn't work," even though "it helps."

Another kind of peace the world gives, continued the pope, "is that of power." So you come to think: "I've got power, I'm secure, I command this, I command that, I'm respected; I'm at peace." That was the situation of King Herod. But "when the wise men arrived and told him that the king of Israel was born," at that very moment "his peace vanished at once." That proves that "the peace of power doesn't work: a coup can take it from you in a flash!"

A third kind of peace "that the world gives" is that of "vanity," which leads us to tell ourselves: "I'm a highly esteemed person, I have so many assets, I'm a person whom all the world respects and when I go to receptions everyone greets me." But neither is this "a lasting peace," warned Pope Francis, "because today you're respected and tomorrow you're insulted!" The pope invited us to think of "what happened to Jesus: the same people who said one thing on Palm Sunday," welcoming him into Jerusalem, "said something else about him on the next Friday." So "the peace of vanity doesn't work," any more than the other kinds of peace the world offers, because they are "temporary, superficial, and not secure."

But in order to understand what true peace is, we need to go back to Jesus' words: "I leave you peace, I give you my peace. I do not give it to you as the world gives it." So what is the peace of Jesus like? "It's a person, it's the Holy Spirit," explained the pope. "On the same day as the resurrection," in the upper room, Jesus greets the disciples saying, "Peace be with you, receive the Holy Spirit." So the peace of Jesus "is a person, a great gift." For "when the Holy Spirit is in our hearts, no one can take that peace away. No one! It's lasting peace!"

So what is "our work" to be done with this great gift? We must "guard that peace," recommended the pope. Indeed, it's "a great peace, a peace that doesn't belong to me but to someone else who gives it to me, someone else who is within my heart, who stays with me all through my life and whom the Lord has given to me."

"How is this peace of the Holy Spirit received?" the pope went on to ask. There were two answers. First, "it's received in baptism, because the Holy Spirit comes, and also at confirmation, because the Holy Spirit comes then." And "it's received as a child receives a present." Jesus himself said: if you don't receive the kingdom of God like a child you will not enter the kingdom of heaven." So "Jesus' peace is to be received without conditions, with an open heart, as a great gift."

The bishop of Rome repeated, "it's the peace of the Holy Spirit." It's up to us "to guard it, not to imprison it, but to feel it, ask for help: he is within us." To the possible objection "there are so many problems," the pope responded with Jesus' own words: "Do not let your hearts be troubled and do not let them be afraid." Indeed, it's the Lord himself who comforts us: "If you have this peace of the Spirit, if you have the Spirit within you and are aware of it, do not let your heart be troubled, you are secure!"

St. Paul too, the pope explained, "told us that in order to enter the kingdom of heaven it is necessary to undergo many trials." Experience confirms that "we all have plenty of trials, some small and some great. All of us!" But the peace of Jesus reassures us, "Do not let your hearts be troubled." Indeed, "the presence of the Spirit brings peace to our hearts, so that they are aware but not anesthetized with that peace which only God's presence gives us."

To check what kind of peace we experience, suggested the pope, "we can ask ourselves some questions: Do I believe that the Holy Spirit is within me? Do I believe that the Lord has given him to me? Do I receive him as a gift, as a child receives a present, with an open heart? Do I guard the Holy Spirit who is in me in order not to distress him?" However, said the pope, there's also an opposite question: "Do I prefer the peace that the world gives me, the peace of money, the peace of power, the peace of vanity?" "These kinds of peace," he repeated, "are 'peace' with fear, always":

the fear that they will come to an end. "The peace of Jesus is lasting; all that's needed is to receive it like a child and keep it." Pope Francis' concluding prayer was: "May the Lord help us to understand these things."

Jesus' Work

Thursday, May 22, 2014
John 15:9-11

"Peace, love, and joy" are "the three key words" that Jesus entrusted to us. It's the Holy Spirit who makes them happen in our lives, but not according to the world's criteria.

The true Christian meaning of the words peace, love, and joy was the theme of Pope Francis' homily at the Mass celebrated on Thursday morning, May 22, in the chapel of St. Martha's House. He took his cue from the prayer read at the beginning of the Mass: "O God, who by your grace made us who were sinners become just, and us who were unhappy become blessed, safeguard your gift in us," that is, the Holy Spirit. In fact, explained the pope, in this prayer "we reminded the Lord of his work in us: 'Made us who were sinners become just, and us who were unhappy become blessed.'" Yes, he declared, "that's the work Jesus has done" and today we "remember it with gratitude." But as well as that, we ask him also to "safeguard his gift, the present he has given us": the Holy Spirit. So we don't say "safeguard us but safeguard your gift."

That's important because, explained the pope, "in his farewell speech during his last days before he went away into heaven, Jesus spoke about so many things," but always bearing on the same point, represented by "three key words: peace, love, and joy."

"We've already reflected" on the first of these, peace, the pope reminded us, at Mass the day before yesterday, agreeing that the Lord "doesn't give us peace as the world gives it; he gives us another peace: a lasting peace!" As for the second of these key words, "love," the pope said, "Jesus had so often said that the commandment is to love God and love our neighbor." "He spoke about it on various occasions," when "he taught us how we should love God rather than idols." And also "how we should love our neighbor." Jesus sums all this up in the "protocol" in chapter 25 of Matthew's gospel, "which we will all be judged on." There the Lord explains "how we should love our neighbor."

But in the gospel passage in today's liturgy (John 15:9-11), "Jesus tells us something else about love: not only must we love but abide in my love." In fact, "the Christian vocation is to abide in God's love, living and breathing that oxygen, living on that air." So we must "abide in God's love." With that statement the Lord "plumbs the depth of his speech on love. And then he goes on."

What is God's love like? Pope Francis answered in Jesus' own words: "As the Father has loved me, so I have loved you." So, it's "love that comes from the Father," and "the loving relationship between Jesus and the Father" becomes "a loving relationship between Jesus and us." Thus "he asks us to abide in that love which comes from the Father." Then "the apostle John goes on to tell us how we must give that love to others," but first and foremost "to abide in love." So this is "the second word" that Jesus leaves with us.

How do we abide in love? Once again the pope answered the question with the Lord's own words: "If you keep my commandments, you will abide in my love, just as I have kept my Father's commandments and abide in his love." That's it: "keeping the commandments" is "the sign that we are abiding in Jesus' love." The pope exclaimed, "That's a beautiful thing. I follow the commandments in my life!" So much so that "when we abide in love the commandments follow of their own accord, from love." For "love leads us to fulfill the commandments quite naturally," because "love's root thrives on the commandments" and the commandments are "the links" in "this love that comes" in the chain connecting the Father, Jesus, and us.

The third word mentioned by the pope was "joy." He recalled Jesus' words in the day's gospel: "I have said these things so that my joy may be in you, and that your joy may be full." Pope Francis said that "joy is the sign of a Christian; a Christian without joy is either not a Christian or sick," his Christian health "is not good." He added, "I said once that there are Christians with faces like peppers pickled in vinegar: always with sour red faces and souls like that too. That's horrible!" These people "aren't Christians" because "a Christian without joy isn't a Christian."

Actually, for a Christian joy is also present "in pain, troubles, even in persecution." Here the pope asked us to look at the martyrs of the early church—like Saints Felicity, Perpetua, and Agnes—who went to their martyrdom as if they were going to their wedding." So that's "the great Christian joy," which "is also what safeguards peace and safeguards love."

Thus, three key words: peace, love, and joy. But, advised the pope, we need to understand their true meaning properly. For they don't come "from the world" but from the Father. Besides, he explained, it's the Holy Spirit "who makes this peace, who makes this love that comes from the Father; who makes the love between the Father and the Son which then comes to us; it's the Holy Spirit who gives us joy." Yes, he said, "it's the Holy Spirit, always him: the one so often forgotten in our lives!" Turning to those present, the pope said he would like to ask—but "I won't!"—how many of you pray to the Holy Spirit. "No, don't put up your hands!" he added at once with a smile. The point, he repeated, is that the Holy Spirit really is "the forgotten one!" But "he's the gift that gives us peace, that teaches us to love and fills us with joy."

In conclusion, the pope repeated the prayer from the beginning of the Mass in which "we asked the Lord to safeguard your gift!" Together, he said, "we asked the Lord for the grace always to safeguard the Holy Spirit in us, that Spirit who teaches us to love, fills us with joy, and gives us peace."

From Sadness to Joy

Friday, May 30, 2014
Acts 18:9-18; John 16:20-23

"Don't be afraid," especially at difficult times. That was Pope Francis' message during the Mass celebrated on Friday, May 30, in the chapel of St. Martha's Guest House. A message of hope, which impels us to be brave and to have "peace of soul" even during trials—illness, persecution, everyday family problems—certain that afterwards we will experience real joy, because "after the darkness the sun always shines."

The pope began with the witness of St. Paul—a "very brave" man—presented in the Acts of the Apostles (18:9-18). Paul, he explained, "did such a lot, because he had the power of the Lord, he had his vocation to advance the church, to preach the gospel." However, even he sometimes felt afraid. So that one night the Lord expressly told him in a vision "not to be afraid."

Even St. Paul "experienced what happens to all of us in our lives," that is, "he felt some fear." Fear which may lead us to review our Christian life, perhaps wondering whether amid so many problems, "mightn't it be better to lower our sights a bit," become "less Christian," seeking "a compromise with the world," so that "things wouldn't be so difficult."

But that reasoning didn't apply to St. Paul, who "knew that

what he was doing didn't please either the Jews or the Gentiles." The Acts of the Apostles tells us the consequences: he was brought before the courts, then there were "persecutions and problems." All this, the pope continued, brings us back to "our own fears, our own dismay." We have to ask ourselves whether being afraid is a Christian thing. Besides, recalled the pope, "Jesus himself felt afraid. Think of the prayer in Gethsemane: 'Father, take away this cup from me.' He suffered anguish." He speaks about this in his farewell speech to his disciples in John's gospel (16:20-23), when he tells them clearly, "You will weep and mourn, but the world will rejoice." As well as that, they will make fools of you.

Something which happened quite quickly. "Think, for example," remarked the bishop of Rome, "of those spectacles in the Colosseum, with the early martyrs who were led "to die for people's entertainment." People said, "These idiots who believed in the Risen One are now ending up like that!" For so many the martyrdom of Christians "was a show: let's see how they die!" Thus what Jesus had said to the disciples happened: "The world will rejoice" while "you will be sad."

So there's "a Christian's fear, a Christian's sadness." Besides, explained the pope, "we must tell ourselves the truth: not all Christian life is a party. Not all of it! We weep, we so often weep!" There are so many difficult situations in life, "when you are ill, when you have family problems, with your son, with your daughter, your wife, or your husband. When you see your wages won't last till the end of the month, or you have a sick child, or you can't pay the mortgage and you lose your home." We have "so many problems." Nevertheless, "Jesus tells us: don't be afraid!"

There's also "another sadness," added Pope Francis: the one "that comes to all of us when we are going down the wrong path." Or when, "to put it simply, we buy, we go out to buy joy, worldly pleasure, which is sinful." The result is that "there's an emptiness inside us; we feel sad." And that's "the sadness of wrongful pleasure."

But although the Lord doesn't shirk sadness, he doesn't leave us with that word alone. Read on and he says, "But if you are faithful, your sadness will turn to joy." That's the key point: "Christian joy is hopeful joy. But at the time of trial we don't see it." Actually, it's "a joy that is purified by trials, even everyday trials." The Lord says, "Your sadness will turn to joy." That's not an easy saying to understand, admitted the pope. It can be seen, for example, "when you go and visit a sick person, who is suffering greatly, to tell them: courage, courage, tomorrow you will have joy!" It's a matter of making that suffering person feel "as Jesus made them feel." It's "an act of faith in the Lord," and so it is for us "when we are really in the dark and can't see anything." That makes us say: "I know, Lord, this sadness will turn to joy. I don't know how, but I know it will!"

During these days, observed the pope, the church in the liturgy is celebrating the moment when "the Lord went away and left the disciples on their own." At that moment, "perhaps some of them felt afraid." But all of them felt "hope, hope that their fear, their sadness, would turn to joy." And "in order to make us realize this is true, the Lord gives the example of a woman in labor," explaining: "Yes, it's true when she's in labor a woman suffers a lot but when she has her baby with her she forgets" all her suffering. And "what remains is joy," the joy "of Jesus; a joy purified in the fire of trials, persecutions, all that we have to undergo to be faithful." This "is the joy that remains, a joy that is hidden at some moments in life, joy we don't feel during the bad times, but which comes later." For it is "joy in hope."

So that's "the church's message for today: not to be afraid," to be "brave in suffering and think that after it the Lord will come, joy will come, after the darkness the sun shines." The pope prayed that "the Lord give all of us this joy in hope." He explained that peace "is the sign that we have this joy in hope." In particular, so many "sick people coming to the end of their lives, and suffering," are witnesses to that "peace of soul." For, the pope concluded, "peace is the seed of joy, is joy in hope." For if "you have peace of soul at dark times, difficult times, times of persecution, when they're all are enjoying your suffering," it's a clear sign that "you have the seed of that joy in you which will come afterwards."

Marriage and Threefold Love

Monday, June 2, 2014
John 16:29-33

The Mass celebrated on Monday morning, June 2, in the chapel of St. Martha's Guest House was a small party for fifteen married couples on their wedding anniversary. Taking his cue from the experience of these families, the pope pointed out the three essential features of the sacrament of marriage and "Jesus' love for the church as her bridegroom," that is, "for all of us": faithfulness, endurance, and fruitfulness.

His reflection on love began from Jesus' farewell speech to the apostles, related in John's gospel (16:29-33). Jesus, explained the pope, "returns to the same subject: the world, the spirit of the world, which does us harm, and the Spirit that Jesus brings, the Spirit of the Beatitudes, the Spirit of the Father." He says expressly, "The Father is with me." That's why he "conquers the world."

"The Father sent Jesus to us," declared the bishop of Rome, because "he so loved the world that, in order to save it he sent his Son, through love." So "Jesus is sent through love and Jesus himself loves." But what is Jesus' love? "Sometimes," he noted, "we've read silly things about the love of Jesus. But Jesus' love is great!" In particular, he pointed out that "Jesus' love was threefold."

First, Jesus "greatly loves the Father in the Holy Spirit." This is a "mysterious" and "eternal" love. So "we can't imagine how great, how beautiful that love is." We can "only ask for the grace to be able to see it one day, when we get there." "Second, Jesus loves his mother." We see that "at the end, although he was in such pain, suffering so much, on the cross he thought of his mother and said: 'Take care of her!'" Third, "Jesus loves the church, his bride, who is beautiful, holy, also sinful, but he loves her just the same."

The presence of the fifteen couples inspired the pope in the second part of his meditation. "When St. Paul refers to the sacrament of marriage," he explained, "he calls it a great sacrament, because Jesus has wedded his church and every Christian marriage is a reflection of that wedding of Jesus with the church."

The pope then confessed he would like to ask each of the couples to tell "what happened during that time, their sixty, fifty, or twenty years of marriage." Then he added at once, "But we wouldn't finish even by midday: so we won't do that!" However, he continued, "we can say something about Jesus the bridegroom's love for the church." It's a love that has "three features: it's faithful; it's enduring, never growing tired of loving his church; and it's fruitful."

First of all "it's faithful love. Jesus is faithful," as St. Paul also reminds us. "Faithfulness," declared the pope, "is the essence of Jesus' love. Jesus' love for his church is faithful. That faithfulness throws light on marriage: love must be faithful, always!" The pope recognized that "there are bad times, sometime there are quarrels. But in the end you make up, ask for forgiveness, and love carries on in the marriage, like Jesus' love for the church."

So married life is "also enduring love," because if that determination is lacking "love can't carry on." You need "endurance in love, in the good times and the difficult times, when there are problems with the children, problems with money." Even in these situations "love perseveres, it always carries on, trying to sort things out to save the family." Turning again to the married couples present, especially those celebrating their sixtieth wedding anniversary, the bishop of Rome remarked that the experience of endurance is beautiful and we see it in "that man and that woman who get up every morning and carry on with the family."

The pope then described fruitfulness as "the third feature of Jesus' love for his bride, the church. Jesus' love makes his bride fruitful, makes the church fruitful with new children, baptisms. The church grows with that fruitfulness resulting from Jesus' love as her bridegroom." But "sometimes the Lord doesn't send children: it's a trial." And "there are other trials: when a child is sick, so many problems." But "these trials deepen the marriage when the couple looks to Jesus and draws strength from the fruitfulness of Jesus with his church, Jesus' love for his church."

Then Pope Francis reminded us "that Jesus doesn't like those marriages which don't want children, that want to remain childless." They are the product of the "culture of affluence from ten years ago," according to which "it's better not to have children, so you can go on holiday round the world, you can have a house in the country and live in comfort!" It's a culture that suggests "it's easier to have a doggy and a couple of cats," so then "your love goes to the two cats and the doggy." But by doing this, "in the end the marriage reaches a lonely old age, and feels bereft; it's not fruitful, it isn't like Jesus with his church."

In conclusion, the pope prayed for the married couples, asking "the Lord to make your marriage beautiful, with crosses to bear, but beautiful like that of Jesus and the church: faithful, enduring, and fruitful."

A Good Advocate

Tuesday, June 3, 2014
Acts 20:17-27; John 17:1-11

We have the best defense counsel, who "doesn't speak much but loves us" and "at this very moment" is praying for each one of us, showing "his wounds to the Father" to remind him of "the price paid to save us." This certainty that "Jesus is praying for us" was the theme of Pope Francis' homily at the Mass celebrated on Tuesday, June 3, in the chapel of St. Martha's Guest House.

"I pray for them; I am not praying for the world, but for those you gave me, because they are yours," are the words of Jesus in his farewell speech, as related in John's gospel (17:1-11). However, the pope noted, the first reading in today's liturgy gives us another "farewell speech." The Acts of the Apostles (20:17-27) tells us that from Miletus Paul sends a message to Ephesus, asking the elders of the church to meet him to say goodbye.

Paul tells them that he doesn't know what will happen to him. "I only know," he says, "that the Holy Spirit testifies to me in every city that imprisonment and persecutions await me." The story goes on to tell us that "they all burst out weeping; they embraced Paul and kissed him, grieving especially because he had told them they would not see his face again. Then they brought him to the ship." But Paul encourages them to carry on, to preach the gospel, not to grow weary.

What Jesus says, noted the pope, is also "a farewell speech before he set out for Gethsemane to begin his passion." And "the disciples are sad" for that reason. But "one small phrase in Jesus' speech makes us stop to think." Actually, Jesus "speaks to his Father in that farewell speech and says, 'I pray for them.'" So "Jesus prays for us." A fact that might seem "rather strange," because "we think it's right to pray to Jesus and Jesus gives us grace. But Jesus prays for us! Jesus praying, Jesus the God-man praying! He prays for us—he prays for me, he prays for you, he prays for each one of us."

Actually, the bishop of Rome continued, Jesus had "already said so clearly to Peter." He assured him that he had prayed "that your faith might not fail." The pope recalled that Jesus also "prays for Lazarus before his tomb." And in his "farewell speech he prays for all the disciples who will come and who will believe" in him. "He doesn't pray for the world but he prays for them," telling the Father that his prayer is "for those you have given me, because they are yours." So Jesus reminds us that "we all belong to the Father and he prays for us to the Father."

"In chapter 8 of his letter to the Romans," the pope explained, "St. Paul tells us that it's a prayer of intercession." So "today while we are here praying, Jesus is praying for us, praying for his church." And "the apostle John" assures us that when we sin we know that "we have an advocate with the Father: someone who prays for us, defends us before the Father, justifies us."

It's important, said the pope, "to think a lot about that truth, that reality: at this very moment Jesus is praying for me. I can carry on with my life because I have an advocate who is defending me. If I am guilty, if I have many sins," Jesus "is a good defense counsel and he will speak to the Father about me."

"To stress that he's the first advocate he tells us, 'I will send you another counselor, another advocate.' But Jesus is the first one. He prays for me, in that prayer of intercession which Jesus is offering now for each one of us since his ascension into heaven." So just as "when in the parish or at home or in the family we need something or we have some problems, we say 'pray for me,' we should say the same to Jesus: 'Lord Jesus, pray for me.'"

How does Jesus pray today? "I don't think he says a lot to the Father, he loves," replied the pope. He added: "But there's one thing that Jesus does today, I'm sure he does: he shows the Father his wounds. Jesus with his wounds prays for us. It's as if he were saying: 'Father, that's the price! Help them, keep them, they are your children whom I have saved.'"

Otherwise, said Pope Francis, "it wouldn't be possible to understand why after the resurrection Jesus had that glorious body, supremely beautiful: there were no bruises on it, no marks of his flogging; it was beautiful, but his five wounds were still there." For "Jesus wanted to carry them to heaven in order to pray for us, to show the Father the price," as if to say: "That's the price, so now don't leave them on their own, help them!"

"We have to have faith," the pope continued, "that at this moment Jesus is interceding for us with the Father, for each one of us. When we pray we ask, Jesus help me, Jesus give me strength, solve this problem, forgive me!" Praying like that, he said, "is good," but at the same time we must not forget also to say: "Jesus, pray for me, show the Father your wounds, which are also mine; they are the wounds of my sin, the wounds of my problem at this moment." So Jesus is "the intercessor who shows his wounds to the Father; that is happening now at this moment."

The pope concluded by repeating Jesus' words to Peter, his prayer that "your faith may not fail." In the certainty that he's praying in the same way for "each one of us: 'I pray for you brother, sister, I pray for you that your faith may not fail!'" Therefore we must "trust that prayer of Jesus, showing his wounds to the Father."

The Church Isn't a Lodging House

Thursday, June 5, 2014
John 17:20-26

"Uniformists, alternativists, and advantagists" are the three neologisms coined by Pope Francis—"somewhat butchering the Italian language," as he himself admitted—to describe three categories of Christians who create divisions in the church. The pope spoke about them this morning, Thursday, June 5, during the Mass in the chapel of St. Martha's Guest House.

Taking his cue from John's gospel (17:20-26), the pope considered the image of "Jesus praying. He prays for his disciples; he prays for all those who will come, who will come from the apostles' preaching; he prays for the church. And what does the Lord ask the Father?" The pope's answer was "for the unity of the church: that the church may be one, that there may be no divisions, no quarrels." That unity, he commented, "needs the Lord to pray for it, because church unity isn't an easy matter." Then he referred to "all those" who "say they belong to the church but only have one foot in the door," while everything else remains "outside."

"For these people," Pope Francis explained, "the church isn't their home." They are people who live like lodgers: "sometimes here and sometimes not." So "there are types of people who lodge in the church but don't think of it as home."

Among these, the bishop of Rome pointed out three categories, beginning with "those who want everyone to be the same in the church": the "uniformists," who want "to make everything uniform, everyone the same." Such people have been there "from the beginning," that is, "since the Holy Spirit wanted to bring Gentiles into the church," recalled the pope, referring to those who held that before they could belong to the church Gentiles had to become Jews. That shows uniformity goes together with rigidity. Pope Francis made a point of calling these Christians "rigid," because "they don't have that freedom given by the Holy Spirit. They confuse what Jesus preached in the gospel" with "their own doctrine of sameness," whereas "Jesus never wanted his church to be rigid." So people like that "don't fit into the church because of their rigidity. They call themselves Christians, but their rigid attitude distances them from the church."

As for the second group, the "alternativists," the bishop of Rome described them as those who think, "I belong to the church, but with this idea, this ideology." They set conditions and "so they're only partial members of the church." They "have one foot in and one foot out of the church; they're lodgers in the church," but they don't feel it's their home. Such people have also been present from the beginning of the gospel preaching, as we see from "the Gnostics, whom the apostle John lambastes so strongly: 'we are . . . yes, yes, we're Catholics but with these ideas.'" They seek an alternative, because they don't share the common sense of the church.

Lastly, the third group consists of those who "seek advantages." They "go to church but for personal advantage and end up doing business in the church." They're profiteers who have also been present from the beginning: like Simon Magus, Ananias, and Sapphira, who "took advantage of the church for their own profit." Turning to the present day, Pope Francis denounced such people who are found regularly "in parishes or dioceses, in religious orders," making themselves out to be "church benefactors." We've seen so many of them, he said. "They paraded themselves as benefactors but at the end of the day they were out for their own profit on the quiet." Naturally, they "don't feel the church is their mother."

However, the message of Jesus is quite different, continued to the pope. To all these types of people, Jesus says: "The church isn't rigid, she's free! In the church there are so many gifts, there's a great diversity of people and gifts of the Spirit. Jesus says that in the church you must give your heart to the gospel, to what the Lord taught, and not find an alternative for yourself! The Lord tells us, if you want to belong to the church," do it "for love, to give everything, your whole heart, and not to do business for your own profit." Indeed, "the church isn't a lodging house," for those who "want to do their own thing." On the contrary, "it's a home to live in."

To those who say that "it's not easy" to have both feet in the church, because "there are so many temptations," the bishop of Rome recalled the one who "creates unity in the church, unity in diversity, freedom, and generosity," that is to say, the Holy Spirit, whose specific "task" is to "create harmony in the church." For "unity in the church is harmony. We are all different, we're not all the same, thank God," for otherwise, he joked, "it would be hell!" But "we are all called to be receptive to the Holy Spirit." That's the virtue which will stop us from becoming rigid, or becoming "alternativists" or "advantagists" or profiteering in the church. We must welcome the Holy Spirit, the one who "makes the church."

It's that welcome which changes the church from a "lodging house" into a house where everyone feels at home. "I'm at home," explained the pope, "because it's the Holy Spirit who gives me this grace." Hence the invitation to ask during the Mass for "the grace of unity in the church, to be brothers and sisters in unity," feeling "we are at home. Unity in the diversity of each one of us," but "free diversity" without setting conditions. "May the Lord send us the Holy Spirit," was Pope Francis' final invocation, "and create that harmony in parishes, dioceses, and movements, because as one of the church fathers said, 'The Spirit himself is harmony.'"

You Never Forget Your First Love

Friday, June 6, 2014
John 21:15-19

You never forget your first love. That also goes for bishops and priests, who must always remember the beauty of their first meeting with Jesus. Then they must be shepherds who follow the

Lord step by step, without worrying about how their own lives will end. These were the essential points of the ministry of bishops and priests that Pope Francis pointed out during the Mass celebrated on the morning of Friday, June 6, in the chapel of St. Martha's House.

The cue for his meditation was the conversation between Jesus and Peter at the end of John's gospel (21:15-19). It's one of Jesus' "beautiful" conversations, following those he had with "the blind man, the Samaritan woman, and the sick man in the pool." His conversation with Peter is "calm"; it takes place "after the resurrection," and also "after a good breakfast." In this gospel passage the pope told us he also found "the conversational style that we priests and bishops should have with the Lord." So "for our conversation with Jesus" he proposed four points for reflection.

John tells us that "the Lord asks Peter three times whether he loves him, whether he's devoted to him." That means, explained the bishop of Rome, that "the love the Lord asks for from a bishop or priest is greater than from others: it's unique, always more." The third time Jesus asked him, noted the pope, Peter "felt hurt, perhaps because he was remembering when he had denied Jesus. But he's even more hurt by the doubt: why are you asking me this?"

The answer is plain: the Lord "wanted to take him back to that first afternoon, when he met Peter's brother Andrew," who then met Peter and told him, "We've found the Messiah!" In a word, Jesus wanted to take Peter back to "that first love." So "when the Lord asks us priests if we love him, he wants to take us back to that first love." The pope then referred to the book of Jeremiah: "I remember the devotion of your youth, your love as a bride, how you followed me in the wilderness" (2:2).

So it's about returning to "that first love which we all felt." For "the Lord wants us to remember that first love in order to renew our love today."

So many married couples "come from their parishes" to the morning Mass at St. Martha's, said the pope. "They're celebrating their fiftieth or sixtieth wedding anniversary." And "I always ask them: so how's it been?" They give "all kinds of answers: one says one thing and another says another . . .!" But one thing they always say: "We're happy!" Once, recalled the pope, both the husband and wife who were celebrating their sixtieth wedding anniversary told me: "We've quarreled" but we are still "as much in love as on the first day."

It's the same question that bishops and priests should ask themselves in order to tell how they still love Jesus today: "Am I still as much in love as on the first day? Or do work and worries make me look to other things and rather forget about love?" In marriage, the pope admitted, quarreling is normal. But "where there's no love there's no quarreling; you break up." So that's the reason why Jesus asks Peter those three questions, "to take him back to that first love." For we should "never forget that first love, never!"

The second point that arises from John's story is the invitation "feed them, be a shepherd!" Perhaps, the pope noted, someone might object: "But Lord, you know, I have to study because I want to become an intellectual in philosophy, theology, patrology . . ." But the answer to those thoughts is "Be a shepherd, the rest will come later! Feed them! With theology, philosophy, patrology, with whatever you're studying, but feed them. Be a shepherd!"

Besides, explained the pope, "the Lord has called us for this." The laying on of "the bishop's hands on our heads is to make us become shepherds." So after the questioning about that "first love," here's a second question that's useful to bishops and priests in an examination of conscience: "Am I a shepherd or am I an employee in that NGO called 'church'?" That's a question we should all ask ourselves, said the pope, and we should answer ourselves with Jesus' exhortation: "Feed! Feed them! Go on!"

The third point relates to another question, the one which Peter asks Jesus about the apostle John: What about him? How will he end up? That, said the pope, is "an interesting question," which "Peter asks out of curiosity, after that conversation. He then looks at John: what will happen to him?"

Basically, "the apostles asked Jesus the same question on the very day of the ascension: Is the triumph coming now?" As if to say, "How will this first love end that has gone so far? How will this shepherding end? Will it end in glory, in majesty?" The answer is very different: "No, brother, it will end in a more common way, sometimes an even more humiliating one." Perhaps, said Pope Francis, "it will end in bed and someone will feed you, dress you, as you lie there helpless and ill." There's no use in repeating "But, Lord, I've done this for you"; I've felt "great love, I've fed your sheep, as you told me, and must I end up like this?" Yes, explained the pope, we have to "end up as he did! That love dies like a grain of wheat and then the fruit will come afterwards. But I won't see it!"

The fourth and last point is "a stronger word: follow me!" That's what Jesus tells us "if we've lost our way and don't know how to respond about love, don't know how to respond about shepherding or don't feel certain that the Lord won't leave us on our own at life's hardest moments, in sickness." That "follow me!" said the pope, must be "our certainty," in the footsteps of Jesus. "That's the way to go."

Pope Francis concluded with a prayer "for bishops and priests: may the Lord give us all the grace always to find or always to remember our first love; to be shepherds; not to be ashamed of ending up in a humiliating bed" or losing our minds. A prayer to the Lord "always to give us the grace to walk behind Jesus," in the footsteps of Jesus, and thus give us "the grace to follow him."

THE CHRISTIAN'S IDENTITY CARD

Monday, June 9, 2014
MATTHEW 5:1-12

The Beatitudes are "the Christian's identity card." So said Pope Francis in his homily during the Mass celebrated on Monday morning, June 9, in the chapel of St. Martha's Guest House. He invited us to reread those pages of the gospel several times in order to try to really live by that "holiness program," which goes "against the tide" of the way of the world.

The pope went over the day's gospel passage (Matthew 5:1-12) point by point. Taking the Beatitudes, he set them in the context of everyday life. Jesus, he explained, speaks "in all simplicity" and makes a kind of "paraphrase, a gloss on the two great commandments: love the Lord and love your neighbor." So "if one of us asks the question, 'What must we do to become a good Christian?'" the answer is simple: you have to do what Jesus says in his beatitudes.

The pope admitted they go "rather against the tide" of what "we usually hear, what is done in the world." For the Lord "knows where sin is, where grace is, and he well knows the ways that lead you to sin and that lead you to grace." That's the meaning of his words "blessed are the poor in spirit," that is, "poverty against wealth."

"Rich people," explained the bishop of Rome, "usually feel secure in their wealth. Jesus himself said so in his parable about the barn," with that man who felt so secure and proud and didn't realize he might die that very day.

"Wealth," he added, "doesn't guarantee you anything. Besides, when the heart is wealthy, it's so self-satisfied that it has no room for God's word." That's why Jesus says, "Blessed are the poor in spirit, who have hearts poor enough for the Lord to enter." And again: "Blessed are those who mourn, for they will be comforted."

On the other hand, noted the pope, "the world tells us that joy, happiness, pleasure are the good things in life!" It "ignores or looks the other way when there are problems of sickness, family troubles." Actually, "the world doesn't want to weep: it prefers to ignore painful situations, to cover them up." Whereas "only those who see things as they are, and weep in their hearts are happy and will be comforted" with the comfort Jesus brings, not that of the world.

"Blessed are the gentle," is a strong expression, especially "in this world which has been warlike from the beginning; a world where there is fighting everywhere, where hatred is everywhere." But "Jesus says: no wars, no hatred! Peace, gentleness!" Someone might object: "If I'm that gentle in life, people will think I'm an idiot." Perhaps they will, said the pope, but "let them think that, but you be gentle because by that gentleness you will inherit the earth!"

"Blessed are those who hunger and thirst for justice" is another great declaration by Jesus, addressed to those who "struggle for justice, for there to be justice in the world." The reality shows us, noted the bishop of Rome, "how easy it is to become involved in corrupt cliques," to play "the game of *do ut des* ['tit for tat' or 'scratch my back and I'll scratch yours']," where "it's all just business." He added: "How many people suffer from those injustices!" Against this, "Jesus tells us blessed are those who fight against such injustices." So, the pope said, "we see how this teaching goes against the tide" of "what the world says."

Then: "Blessed are the merciful for they will receive mercy." This, he explained, is about "those who forgive; they understand the mistakes others make." Jesus "doesn't say: blessed are those who seek revenge, pursue a vendetta," or who say "an eye for an eye, a tooth for a tooth," but he calls those blessed "who forgive, who are merciful." And we must always remember, the pope re-called, that "we are all a company of the forgiven! We've all been forgiven! And the person who forgives is blessed."

Next, "blessed are the pure in heart" is a saying by Jesus refer-ring to those "whose hearts are simple, pure, unsullied: hearts that can love with that purity that is so fine." Then, "blessed are the peacemakers" refers to all the war situations that keep recurring. For us, he admitted, "it's just as common to be warmongers or stirrers of misunderstandings." This happens "when I hear some-thing about someone and I go to someone else and tell it; and I even issue a second, rather enlarged, edition and report that." In short, it's "the world of gossip," consisting of "gossips who don't make peace," who are enemies of peace and certainly not blessed.

Finally, by proclaiming "blessed are those who are persecuted for justice's sake," Jesus recalls "all the persecuted" and those "who are persecuted simply because they fought for justice."

So, said the pope, "that's the life program proposed by Jesus." A program that is "so simple" but at the same time "so hard." Then "if we want more, Jesus also gives us other pointers," in par-ticular "that check list of things we will be judged on in chapter 25 of Matthew's gospel: 'I was hungry and you gave me food; I was thirsty and you gave me drink; I was sick and you took care of me; I was in prison and you visited me.'"

That's the way, he explained, "to live a Christian life on the level of holiness." For, he added, "what the saints did" was live by the Beatitudes and that "check list for the last judgment." They are "few words, simple words, but practical, because Christianity is a practical religion," to be practiced, to do, not just to think about.

Pope Francis' final suggestion was also practical: "Today if you have a little time at home, take up Matthew's gospel, and you will find the Beatitudes at the beginning of chapter 5." Then "in chapter 25 you'll find the other" words of Jesus. "It will do you good," he urged, "to read them once, twice, three times because it's a holiness program."

WHEN HATRED KILLS

Thursday, June 12, 2014
MATTHEW 5:20-26

In order to do justice properly, living by the commandment of love, we have to be realists and be consistent. We must recognize that we are children of the same Father, hence brothers and sisters. These are the three criteria suggested by Pope Francis at the Mass celebrated on Thursday morning, June 12, in the chapel of St. Martha's Guest House.

In the gospel passage for today's liturgy (Matthew 5:20-26), the pope explained, Jesus speaks to us about "how we should love one another." Here are his words: "I tell you, unless your justice exceeds that of the scribes and Pharisees, you will never enter the kingdom of heaven."

So Jesus is telling us "we must be just, we must love our neighbor—a problem for today—but we shouldn't do so like those doctors of the law who had a special philosophy." They spelled out "everything that ought to be done"—regarding themselves as "clever" and "good"—but "then not doing it." That's why "Jesus says of them: do what they say but not what they do." For, he says, "they aren't consistent."

They were people who "knew that the first commandment was to love God; they knew that the second commandment was to love our neighbor." However, "they had so many ifs and buts in their ideas, because they were ideologists." They had a whole system of distinctions in what it means to "love your neighbor."

In the end they reached "an attitude that wasn't love," but rather "indifference toward your neighbor." So Jesus recommends us to go beyond that way of behaving, which "isn't justice but a social balancing act."

In order to do so, said the pope, Jesus suggests "three criteria" to us. The first is "the criterion of sensible realism." For Jesus says, "if you have something against the other person and you can't sort it out and seek a solution," it's a good idea to find a way "at least to come to terms." Above all, the Lord advises, "come to terms with your adversary while you are on the way [to court]." Perhaps "it won't be ideal, but an agreement is a good thing; it's realistic!"

To those who object that "agreements don't last," or even, as the saying goes, "they are made to be broken," the answer is that "the effort to come to agreement" serves to "save such a lot of things: one person takes a step, the other takes another" and "so at least there's peace." Even though, the pope admitted, it may be "a very temporary peace," because it was brokered by an agreement.

In short, "Jesus is a realist" when he tells us "the ability to come to an agreement between each other also means going beyond the justice of the Pharisees and doctors of the law." It's "being realistic in life." So Jesus expressly recommends us to come to "an agreement while we are on the way, in order to put a stop to the dispute and hatred between us. But so often we want to make an end of things, take them to the wire."

"A second criterion that Jesus gives us is the criterion of truth," explained the pope. In fact, there's the commandment not to kill; but "speaking ill of another person is also killing, because there's the same hatred at its root. You haven't got the courage to kill him or you think that's going too far, but you kill him in another way, by gossip, by slander, by libel."

In Matthew's gospel Jesus' words on the subject are plain: "But I say to you that if you are angry with a brother or sister you will be liable to judgment. If you say 'you numbskull!' to a brother or sister you will be liable to the council; and if you say 'you fool!' you will be liable to the hell of fire." So, explained the pope, "when we hear people saying such ugly things," we must always remember that calling someone "numbskull" or "fool" is killing your brother or sister, because insulting "has its root in hatred." Actually, "it derives from the same root as crime: it's hatred!" However, he continued, "insulting other people is very common among us." There are people, he noted, "who have an impressive capacity to express their hatred for someone else." They don't think about the harm that "yelling and badmouthing" do.

The third criterion that Jesus gives us "is the criterion of relationship." We "shouldn't kill our brother or sister," precisely because we are related to them as brothers and sisters and "we have the same Father." We read in the gospel, "I can't go to the Father if I'm not at peace with my brother or sister." Indeed, Jesus says, "So when you are offering your gift at the altar, if you remember that your brother or sister has something against you, leave your gift there before the altar and go; first be reconciled to your brother or sister and then come and offer your gift." So the Lord tells us "not to speak to the Father if you are not at peace with your brother or sister," or "at least have an agreement with them."

The pope summed up: "There you have the three criteria: the criterion of realism, the criterion of consistency, that is, not killing but not insulting either, because insulting is murder, is killing; and the criterion of relationship: I can't speak with the Father if I can't speak with my brother or sister." These are the three criteria for "going beyond the justice of the scribes and Pharisees."

"Not an easy program," the bishop of Rome admitted, "but it's the way Jesus shows us to go." In conclusion, Pope Francis asked the Lord for "the grace to be able to go in peace among ourselves," perhaps "with agreements between us, but always consistently and as brothers and sisters with one Father."

The Still Small Voice

Friday, June 13, 2014
1 Kings 19:9, 11-16

Before giving us a mission the Lord prepares us, testing us by a process of purification and discernment. It was the story of the prophet Elijah that provoked the pope's reflection on that fundamental law of Christian life, during the Mass celebrated on Friday morning, June 13, in the chapel of St. Martha's Guest House.

"In the first reading," said the pope, referring to the passage taken from the first book of Kings (19:9, 11-16), "we heard the story of Elijah: how the Lord prepares a prophet, how he works on the prophet's heart so that he may be faithful to the Lord's word and do what the Lord wants."

The prophet Elijah "was a strong person with great faith. He had berated the people for worshiping both God and idols: if they worshiped idols they didn't rightly worship God! And if they worshiped God, they worshiped idols badly!" That was why Elijah told the people they were limping "with two different opinions"; they were unstable and not firm in their faith. In his mission "Elijah was brave" and in the end he challenged the priests of Baal on Mount Carmel, and he beat them. "To finish the story he killed them all," thus putting an end to idolatry "in that part of the people of Israel." So Elijah "was happy because the power of the Lord was with him."

But, continued the pope, "next day Queen Jezebel—she was the king's wife but she was the one who ruled—threatened him and told him she would kill him." This threat "frightened Elijah so much that he became depressed; he went away and wanted to die." That same prophet, who on the day before "had been so brave and had defeated" the priests of Baal, "today is downhearted. He doesn't want to eat and he wants to die, because he feels so depressed." All that, explained the pope, "because a woman has threatened him." So "the four hundred priests of the idol Baal couldn't scare him, but this woman did!"

That's a story which "shows us how the Lord prepares someone for a mission." Elijah "in his depression goes into the wilderness to die. He lies down to wait for death. But the Lord calls him" and invites him to eat a bit of bread and drink because, he tells him, "he still has a long way to go." So Elijah "eats, drinks, but then lies down again. Once again the Lord calls him: Get up and go!"

The thing is, Elijah "didn't know what to do, but he felt that he should go up the mountain to find God. He was brave, he walked there in humble obedience. For he was obedient." Even in a state of dismay and "feeling so afraid," Elijah "went up the mountain to await God's message, God's revelation. He prayed, because he was good, but he didn't know what would happen. He didn't know, he was there waiting for the Lord."

We read in the Old Testament: "The Lord passed by. And a great and strong wind split the mountains and broke the rocks in pieces before the Lord, but the Lord was not in the wind." Elijah, commented the pope, "realized that the Lord wasn't there." The Bible continues: "After the wind an earthquake; but the Lord was not in the earthquake." So, continued the pope, Elijah "could tell that the Lord was not in the earthquake or the wind." The story in the first book of Kings continues: "After the earthquake a fire, but the Lord was not in the fire. And after the fire, a still small voice." And "when Elijah heard it, he realized" that "it was the Lord passing by. He wrapped his face in his cloak and worshiped the Lord."

Indeed, declared the bishop of Rome, "the Lord was not in the wind, or the earthquake, or the fire, but he was in that still small voice: in peace." Or "as the original puts it in a very beautiful way: the Lord was in 'a resonant whisper of silence.'"

So Elijah "knows how to discern where the Lord is and the Lord prepares him with the gift of discernment." Then he gives him his mission: "You've been tested by depression," feeling low, "by hunger; you've been put to the test of discernment" but now—the Bible tells us—"Go, return on your way to the wilderness of Damascus. When you arrive there, you shall anoint Hazael as king over Aram. Also you shall anoint Jehu son of Nimshi as king of Israel and you shall anoint Elisha."

So that's the mission awaiting Elijah, the pope explained. The Lord made him go through all that long journey to prepare him for his mission. Perhaps, it could be objected, it would have been "much easier to say: you've been so brave to kill those four hundred, so now go and anoint so and so!" Instead, "the Lord prepares his soul, prepares his heart, and prepares him by testing him, prepares him in obedience, and prepares him in endurance."

"That's what Christian life is like," said the pope. In fact, "when the Lord wants to give us a mission, wants to give us a task, he prepares us to do it well," just as "he prepared Elijah." So what's important "isn't that he met the Lord" but "his whole journey to get to the mission the Lord entrusts him with." For "that's just the difference between the apostolic mission that the Lord gives us and a good, honest, human task." For "when the Lord gives us a mission, he always puts us through a process of purification, a process of discernment, a process of obedience, a process of prayer." That, he repeated, "is Christian life"; that is "faithfulness to the whole process, allowing ourselves to be led by the Lord."

We can draw an important teaching from the story of Elijah. The prophet "was afraid, and that's so very human," because Jezebel "was a wicked queen who threatened her enemies." Elijah "is afraid but the Lord is stronger" and makes him understand that "he needs the Lord's help to prepare for his mission." So Elijah "walks, obeys, suffers, discerns, prays, and finds the Lord." Pope

Francis concluded his homily with a prayer: "May the Lord give us the grace to let ourselves be prepared every day on the journey of our life, so that we may bear witness to the salvation of Jesus."

WHEN THE POOR PAY

Monday, June 16, 2014
I KINGS 21:1-16

It's always the poor who pay the price of corruption. Any corruption: corruption of politicians, businessmen, and also by members of the clergy who neglect their "pastoral duties" in order to pursue "power." Once again Pope Francis denounced in strong language "the sin of corruption," committed by "so many of those who have power, material power, political power, or spiritual power." During the Mass celebrated on Monday morning, June 16, at St. Martha's, he invited us to pray, in particular, for "all those many, many people who pay for corruption, who pay for the lives of the corrupt, who are martyrs to political corruption, economic corruption, and church corruption."

Taking his cue from the passage from the first book of Kings (21:1-16), read during the liturgy, the pope recalled the story of Naboth the Jezreelite, who refuses to hand over to King Ahab his vineyard, which he had inherited from his father. For that, at the instigation of Queen Jezebel, he is stoned. "A very sad passage in the Bible," commented the bishop of Rome, noting that the story follows the same structure as that of Jesus' trial and the martyrdom of Stephen. He recalled a sentence from Mark's gospel (10:42): "You know that among the Gentiles those whom they recognize as their rulers lord it over them, and their great ones are tyrants over them."

"This Naboth," said the pope, "is like a martyr of that king, who rules tyrannically and oppresses." In order to get hold of the vineyard, at first Ahab makes Naboth an honest offer: "I'll buy it from you, I'll exchange it for another one." But when the man refuses to give up "his inheritance from his fathers," Ahab goes home "resentful and sullen," behaving almost like a "spoiled child" throwing "a tantrum." At this point his wife Jezebel—"the one who had threatened the prophet Elijah with death after he had killed the priests of Baal"—organizes a show trial with false witnesses and has Naboth killed, allowing her husband to take possession of the vineyard. Ahab does so, noted the pope, "calmly, as if nothing had happened."

This is a story, Francis declared, that "is often repeated by so many who have power—material power, political power, or spiritual power. But it's a sin: it's the sin of corruption." How does someone become corrupt? "He becomes corrupt," said the pope, "in pursuit of his own security. First comfort, money, then power, vanity, pride, and from then on anything, even murder."

"In the newspapers," observed the bishop of Rome, "we so often read: such and such a politician who magically enriched himself has been brought to court. Or that company boss who magically enriched himself by exploiting his workers has been indicted, brought to court. We hear too often about a member of the clergy who has become very rich and abandoned his pastoral duties in order to pursue his own power." So there are "corrupt politicians, corrupt businessmen, and corrupt clerics." They are "everywhere." Because, explained the pope, corruption "is the sin ready to hand for someone who has authority over others, whether it's economic, political, or church authority. We are all tempted to corruption. It's a sin ready to hand." Besides, he added, "when you have authority, you feel powerful; you almost feel you're God." So corruption "is an everyday temptation" into which "a politician, a businessman, or a member of the clergy" may fall.

But, asked Francis, "who pays for that corruption?" Of course, "the one by whom the bribe is handed over" doesn't pay: he's only "the go-between." In fact, said the pope "it's the poor who pay!" It wasn't an accident that Ahab's corruption "was paid for by Naboth, that poor man faithful to his tradition, faithful to his values, faithful to the inheritance he had received from his father."

"If we're talking about corrupt politicians or corrupt businessmen, who pays?" the pope asked again. "Those who pay are hospitals without medicines, the sick who aren't cared for, children without education. They are the Naboths of today, who pay for the corruption of the great." And, he continued, "who pays for the corruption of the clergy? Those who pay are children who don't know how to make the sign of the cross, who don't know their catechism, who are not looked after. Those who pay are the sick who are not visited; those who pay are prisoners who have no pastoral care." In the end it's always the poor who pay for corruption, the "materially poor" and the "spiritually poor."

"But it is not so among you," says Jesus to his disciples, urging those who "have power" to become "servants." Indeed, said Francis, "the only way out of corruption, the only way to overcome the temptation, the sin of corruption, is service. Corruption comes from pride, arrogance. Service makes you humble; it means helping others in humble kindness."

In conclusion, the bishop of Rome stressed the value of Naboth's witness, as he "didn't want to sell his inheritance from his fathers, his ancestors, his values." His witness is all the more significant when we consider that "where there's corruption" the poor often risk losing "their values, because other habits and laws which go against their ancestral values are imposed upon them." Hence the pope's invitation to pray for all those "martyrs to corruption," that "the Lord may draw us closer to them" and give these poor people "the power to carry on" bearing their witness.

Sinners in White Gloves

Tuesday, June 17, 2014
1 Kings 21:17-29

The way out of corruption is to beg for forgiveness, repentance. That was Pope Francis' emphasis when he returned to the subject of corruption this morning, Tuesday, June 17, during the Mass celebrated in St. Martha's chapel. "When we read in the newspapers," he said, "that so and so is corrupt, or some other person is corrupt, that they have committed the crime of corruption and bribery has spread here and there, and a lot of other things about certain clergy," it's "our duty as Christians to ask forgiveness for them," to ask the Lord "to give them the grace to repent, so that they don't die with corrupt hearts." That means "yes, condemn the corrupt; yes, ask for the grace not to become corrupt," but also "pray for the conversion of those who are corrupt!"

The biblical passage in today's liturgy which inspired the pope's reflection tells the story of the killing of Naboth, related in the first book of Kings (21:17-29). Pope Francis pointed out three aspects of the story "which it will do us good to meditate on": the definition of corruption, the fate of the corrupt, and the chance they have to save themselves.

With regard to the first point, the protagonist of the story, the prophet Elijah himself, clearly denounces "what the corrupt person does." He is addressing Ahab, the one responsible for the stoning of Naboth, who had refused to sell him his vineyard: "You have killed and also taken possession . . . You have sold yourself!" In fact, commented the bishop of Rome, "when he sets out on that way of corruption, the corrupt person does one thing today and tomorrow another. He takes life, usurps, and sells himself continually." In practice, he added with a powerful image, "it's as if he'd stopped being a person and become a commodity." So the corrupt person "is a commodity! He buys and sells: 'That man, yes, he costs that much; you can buy him and sell him!' That's the definition: he's a commodity!"

As to the second point—what will the Lord do with the corrupt?—the pope began by recalling the three types of corrupt people mentioned in his homily on the day before: "the corrupt politician, the corrupt businessman, and the corrupt cleric." He explained that "all three harm the innocent, the poor, because it's the poor who pay for the feasting of the corrupt! They pay the bill!" Returning to the question of the fate of the corrupt, he pointed out that in today's reading the Lord himself says "clearly what he will do: 'I will bring disaster on you; I will consume you, and will cut off from Ahab every male, bond or free in Israel . . . because you have provoked me and have caused Israel to sin!'" Indeed, "the corrupt person provokes God and makes the people sin." That's why the Lord uses such strong language about Ahab, the archetype of all the corrupt, when the prophet Elijah prophesies that "in the place where the dogs licked up the blood of Naboth, dogs will also lick up your blood!" It's not accidental, the pope continued, that "when Mary sings of salvation history in her praise song, she says the Lord scatters the proud and puts down the mighty from their seats." Jesus himself explained the reason: "If any one of you causes scandal, it would be better for him to be thrown into the sea." That's because "the corrupt person causes scandal, scandalizes society, scandalizes the people of God." So "the Lord is angry with the corrupt because they cause scandal; they exploit those who can't defend themselves, they enslave them." Like Ahab, "the corrupt sell themselves to do harm, but don't know it; they believe they sell themselves to get more money, more power. But they sell themselves to do harm, to kill."

Of course, said Pope Francis, "when we say, 'This man is corrupt; that woman is corrupt . . . ,'" we must stop to reflect a bit, ask ourselves whether we have proofs for what we are saying. Because, he explained, "saying that this person is corrupt is saying just that; it's saying they're condemned; it's saying that the Lord has thrown them out." By being traitors, people who rob and kill, they risk incurring "God's curse, because they've exploited the innocent, those who can't defend themselves. They've done so wearing white gloves, from a distance, without getting their hands dirty."

However, there is "a way out for the corrupt. Ahab tore his clothes, put on sackcloth and fasted. He put sackcloth over his bare flesh and walked with his head down. He began to do penance." The pope compared Ahab's experience with that of "that man who was so good but who fell into corruption: St. David. David admitted: 'I've sinned!' He wept and did penance; he repented." So "asking for forgiveness" is "the way out for the corrupt, for corrupt politicians, corrupt businessmen, and corrupt clerics." Indeed, "this pleases the Lord." He forgives but he does so "when the corrupt do what Zacchaeus did: 'Lord, I've robbed. I'll give back four times what I robbed!'" Hence the pope's concluding invitation was to pray for all the corrupt, asking forgiveness for them so that they might obtain "the grace of repentance."

TREASURE HUNTING

Friday, June 20, 2014
II KINGS 11:1-4, 9-18, 20; MATTHEW 6:19-23

"**M**oney, vanity, and power" don't make us happy. True treasures, the riches that count, are "love, patience, service to others, and worship of God." That was Pope Francis' message during the Mass celebrated on Friday morning, June 20, in the chapel of St. Martha's Guest House.

The heart of the pope's meditation were the words of Jesus related in Matthew's gospel (6:19-23): "Do not store up for yourselves treasures on earth, where moth and rust consume and where thieves break in and steal; but store up for yourselves treasures in heaven, where neither moth nor rust consumes and where thieves do not break in and steal. For where your treasure is, there will your heart be also." So, the pope commented, "Jesus' advice is simple: don't store up treasures for yourselves on earth! It's prudent advice." That's why Jesus adds: "Look, these things are of no use, so don't waste your time!"

There are three treasures that Jesus warns against on several occasions. "The first treasure is gold, money, wealth," explained the bishop of Rome. Indeed, "you aren't safe with this treasure, because perhaps you will be robbed. You aren't safe with investments: perhaps the stock market will crash and you'll be left with nothing!" So "tell me: does one more dollar make you happier or not?" For, the pope continued, "wealth is a dangerous treasure." Of course, money can also be useful "to do so many good things," for example, "bring up a family." But, he warned, "if you store it up as a treasure, it steals your soul." That's why "in the gospel Jesus keeps returning to it, to wealth, to the danger of wealth, of putting your trust in wealth." He tells us to beware because it's a treasure "that's of no use."

The second treasure the Lord speaks about "is vanity," that is, seeking "to have prestige, to be seen." Jesus always condemns that attitude: "Think of what he tells the doctors of the law when they fast, when they give alms, when they pray in order to be seen." Besides, even "vanity is of no use, it comes to an end. Beauty comes to an end." On that theme the pope quoted an expression—which he called "rather strong"—of St. Bernard's, according to which "your beauty will end up being food for worms."

Pride, power, "is the third treasure" that Jesus calls useless and dangerous. We read about that in the first reading in today's liturgy taken from the second book of Kings (11:1-4, 9-18, 20), which tells the story of the "cruel Queen Athaliah: her great power lasted for seven years, then she was killed." In short, "you're here one day and gone tomorrow," because "power comes to an end. How many great, proud, powerful men and women finished anonymously, in poverty or in prison . . ."

So that's the essence of Jesus' teaching: "Don't store it up! Don't store up money, don't store up vanity, don't store up pride, power! Those treasures are of no use!" But there are other treasures which you should store up, declared the pope. In fact, "there are some treasures which it's good to store up." Jesus tells us so in the same gospel passage: "Where your treasure is, there will your heart be also." That's "Jesus' message: have a free heart." But "if your treasure lies in wealth, in vanity, power or pride, your heart will be chained to them; your heart will become a slave to wealth, vanity or pride."

So Pope Francis urged us to have "a free heart," because "Jesus expressly speaks about freedom of heart." And "you can only have a free heart with the treasures of heaven: love, patience, service of others, worship of God." These "are the real wealth that can't be robbed." Other wealth—money, vanity, power—"weigh down the heart, chain it, don't give it freedom."

So we must look to store up true wealth, which "frees the heart" and makes you "a man or woman with the freedom of the children of God." We read about it in the gospel that "if your heart is enslaved, your eye won't be light, your heart won't be light." Indeed, stressed Pope Francis, "an enslaved heart isn't light: it's dark!" So "if we store up earthly treasures, we store up darkness which is of no use, which gives us no joy. Above all, it gives us no freedom."

But "a free heart is a light heart, which gives light to others," said the bishop of Rome. "It enables us to see the way that leads to God." It's "a light heart that isn't chained, a heart that goes ahead, and also ages well, because it ages like good wine. When good wine ages it's a good wine that has aged!" And vice versa, he added, "a heart that isn't light is like bad wine: time passes and it deteriorates and becomes vinegar."

The pope concluded by inviting us to pray to the Lord "for the spiritual wisdom to know where my heart is, what treasure my heart is attached to." And "may he also give us the power to 'unchain it,' if it's chained, so that it may become free, become light. May he also give us that beautiful happiness of being children of God, which is true freedom."

No One Can Judge

Monday, June 23, 2014
MATTHEW 7:1-5

Those who judge put themselves in God's place and by doing so they're heading for certain defeat in life, because they will be repaid in the same coin. They live in a muddle, mistaking the "speck" in a brother's eye for the "plank" in their own which stops them from seeing. Pope Francis issued an invitation to defend others rather than judging them during the Mass celebrated on Monday morning, June 23, in the chapel of St. Martha's Guest House.

The gospel passage in the day's liturgy (Matthew 7:1-5), the pope noted, shows us Jesus himself "trying to convince us not to judge," a commandment that "he repeats many times." In fact, "judging others leads to hypocrisy." Jesus calls "hypocrites" those who set themselves up to judge. Because, the pope explained, "those who judge make a mistake, they get muddled and are defeated."

Those who judge "always make mistakes." They are mistaken, he said, "because they set themselves in God's place, who is the only judge. They set themselves up in that place and it's the wrong place!" In practice, they believe they have "the power to judge everything: people, lives, everything." And "as well as the capacity to judge," they also claim "the capacity to condemn."

The gospel tells us that "judging others was one of the attitudes of those doctors of the law whom Jesus called 'hypocrites.'" They were people who "judged everything." But the "worst of it" was that by doing so, "they took God's place, who is the only judge." For "when God judges he takes his time, he waits," whereas these men "judge at once. So those who judge are mistaken, simply because they set themselves in a place which doesn't belong to them."

However, said the pope, "not only are they mistaken but they get in a muddle." For "they become so obsessed with the person they want to judge—so completely obsessed—that they lose sleep over the speck in that person's eye." They keep saying, "I want to get rid of that speck!" But they don't realize that "they themselves have a plank" in their own eye. "They get in a muddle" and "believe the plank is that speck." So anyone who judges is someone who "muddles the reality" and is under an illusion.

Not only that. For the pope those who judge "suffer defeat" and can only come to a bad end, "because the same measure will be used to judge them," as Jesus tells us in Matthew's gospel. So "the proud, self-sufficient judges who mistake their place because they set themselves in God's place, are setting themselves up for a fall." What is that defeat? "Being judged by the same measure with which they judge," remarked the bishop of Rome. For "the only one to judge is God and those to whom God gives the power to do so. Others have no right to judge; so the result is muddle, the result is defeat."

On top of all that, the pope continued, "the defeat goes further, because anyone who judges always accuses." In a "judgment against another—the Lord gives us the example of 'the speck in your eye'—there's always an accusation." That's exactly the opposite of what "Jesus does before the Father." In fact, Jesus "never accuses." On the contrary, he defends. He "is the first advocate. Then he sends us a second one, who is the Spirit." Jesus is "the defender: he stands before the Father to defend us from accusations."

But if there's a defender, there's also an accuser. "In the Bible," explained the pope, "the accuser is called the devil, Satan." Jesus "will judge at the end of the world, but meanwhile he intercedes, he defends." John, noted the pope, "says it so well in his gospel: please don't sin, but if anyone sins, know that we have an advocate who defends us before the Father."

So, he declared, "if we want to follow the way of Jesus, we should be defenders of others before the Father, not accusers." We should defend anyone undergoing "something bad" without thinking too much about it. "Go and pray and defend that person before the Father, as Jesus does. Pray for them."

Above all, the pope repeated, "don't judge, because if you do, when you do something bad, you will be judged!" That, he suggested, is something we do well to remember "in everyday life when we feel the urge to judge others, to speak ill of others, which is a kind of judging."

In short, repeated the pope, "those who judge mistake their place; they get in a muddle and suffer defeat." In doing so, "they don't imitate Jesus, who always defends us before the Father: he is counsel for the defense." But anyone who judges "is an imitator of the prince of this world, who always pursues people to accuse them before the Father."

Pope Francis ended by praying to the Lord "to give us grace to imitate Jesus, who is the intercessor, defender, advocate for us and others." And "not to imitate the Other One, who in the end will destroy us."

CHRISTIANS
WHO CAN HUMBLE THEMSELVES

Tuesday, June 24, 2014
ISAIAH 49:1-6; LUKE 1:57-66, 80

Preparing, discerning, decreasing. These three verbs sum up the spiritual experience of St. John the Baptist, the one who preceded the coming of the Messiah by "preaching the baptism of repentance" to the people of Israel. During the Mass celebrated on Tuesday morning, June 24, on the feast of the Birth of the Precursor, Pope Francis took up this threesome as a paradigm of the vocation of any Christian, referring to three expressions of John the Baptist's attitude to Jesus: "After me, before me, far from me."

First of all, John had worked to "prepare the way, without taking anything for himself." The pope reminded us, "he was an important man; people went to look for him, they followed him," because his words "were powerful" like "a sharp sword," according to the word of Isaiah (49:2). The Baptist "reached people's hearts." If "maybe he suffered the temptation to think of himself as important, he didn't fall into it." That's shown in the reply he gave to the doctors who asked him if he was the Messiah: "I am the voice of one crying in the wilderness. I am just a voice, but I have come to prepare the way of the Lord." So his first task was "to prepare the hearts of the people to meet the Lord."

But who is the Lord? The answer to that question gives us "John's second task, which was to discern, among so many good people, who was the Lord." And, the pope observed, "the Spirit revealed it to him." So "he had the courage to say: 'That's the one. He is the lamb of God, who takes away the sins of the world.'" While "during the preparation John had said: 'After me comes one . . .' in his discernment he recognizes and points out the Lord, saying: 'He is . . . before me.'"

Then comes "John's third vocation, which is to decrease." For "from that very moment," the bishop of Rome recalled, "his life began to go down, to decrease, so that the Lord might increase, until in the end he was annihilated." That, noted Pope Francis, was "John's most difficult stage, because the Lord had a style that he hadn't imagined. So when John was in prison," where he had been sent by Herod Antipas, "he suffered not only the darkness of his prison cell, but the darkness in his heart." He was beset by doubts: "But is he the one? Have I made a mistake?" Then, the pope recalled, he sent his disciples to go to Jesus and ask: "Are you really the one or are we to wait for another?"

"John suffered a double humiliation," the bishop of Rome stressed, "the humiliation of his death as the price of a whim," but also the humiliation of not seeing "the history of salvation: he suffered the humiliation of darkness of soul." This man, who "had proclaimed the Lord coming after him," who "had seen him before him," who "had awaited him and been able to recognize him," now "sees Jesus as far away. That promise has receded into the distance. He ends up alone, in the dark, in humiliation." Not because he wallows in suffering, but "because he diminished himself so that the Lord might increase." So John ended up "humiliated but with his heart at peace."

"It's a fine thing," Francis concluded, "to think of the Christian vocation like that." Indeed, "a Christian doesn't proclaim himself, he proclaims someone else; he prepares the way for someone else: the Lord." On top of that, "he must know how to discern, how to discern the truth from what seems like truth but isn't: he must be discerning." Finally, "he must be someone who knows how to humiliate himself so that the Lord may increase, in the hearts and souls of others."

THOSE WHO SPEAK WITHOUT AUTHORITY

Thursday, June 26, 2014
MATTHEW 7:21-29

People need a "good shepherd" who understands them and reaches their hearts. Just like Jesus. He is the one we should follow closely, without being influenced by those who "speak about abstract things or with moral casuistry"; or those who "lack faith and negotiate everything with the political and economic powers"; or the "revolutionaries" who want to engage politically in "so-called wars of liberation"; or the "contemplatives who are remote from the people."

Pope Francis warned against these four attitudes in the Mass celebrated on Thursday, June 26, in the chapel of St. Martha's Guest House. The pope began by pointing out what a lot of people there were who followed Jesus. "Think of the day of the multiplication of the loaves, when there were more than five thousand." These people followed Jesus closely "on his way." The gospel explains that they followed him "because Jesus' words astounded them: their hearts were astounded at hearing something good and great." For Jesus "taught them as one having authority, and not as their scribes." The day's gospel passage from Matthew (7:21-29) speaks of that astonishment.

"The people needed teachers, preachers, doctors with authority," said the pope. Those who "had no authority" spoke, but their words didn't reach the people; "they were remote from the people." The novelty was that "Jesus spoke a language that reached people's hearts, he answered their needs."

Pope Francis then turned to "those scribes who spoke to the people at that time" but "their message didn't reach people's hearts and the people listened and went away." He mentioned four types.

Certainly "the best known group was that of the Pharisees,"

he said, but stressed that "there were also good Pharisees." But "when Jesus refers to the Pharisees, he's talking about the bad ones, not the good ones." They were people who "turned the worship of God, religion, into a collection of commandments." Instead of just ten, "they created more than three hundred!" In short, they "laid this burden on people's shoulders: 'You must do this! You must!'" They reduced faith in the living God to casuistry and ended up in "cruel casuistic contradictions." And "the people respected them, because they were respectful, but they didn't listen to these casuistical preachers."

Another group, continued the pope, "were the Sadducees. They were without faith, they had lost their faith." So "their religious task was to come to agreements with the ruling powers: the political and economic powers." In short, "they were men of power and negotiated with anybody." But "the people didn't follow them" either.

"A third group were the revolutionaries," who at that time were often called Zealots. They were "those who wanted to have a revolution to liberate the people of Israel from the Roman occupation." So "they also included guerrillas." But "the people have good sense and know how to tell when the fruit is ripe and when it isn't." That's why "they didn't follow these Zealots."

Lastly, said the pope, "the fourth group" consisted of good people: the Essenes. "They were monks," he said, "good people who devoted their lives to God; they engaged in contemplation and prayer in monasteries." But "they were remote from the people and the people couldn't follow them."

So, the pope summed up, "these were the voices that reached the people." However, "none of those voices had the power to warm people's hearts." But Jesus did. That's why "the crowds were astounded: they listened to Jesus and their hearts burned," because his message "reached their hearts" and "he taught as one having authority." Indeed, the pope continued, "Jesus came close to the people; Jesus healed their hearts; Jesus understood their difficulties; Jesus wasn't ashamed to talk to sinners, he went looking for them; Jesus enjoyed himself; he liked walking with his people." Jesus himself explained why, "because," said the pope quoting the words of John's gospel, "I am the good shepherd. The sheep hear my voice and follow me."

That's the very reason "why the people followed Jesus: because he was the good shepherd." Certainly, said the bishop of Rome, "he wasn't either a casuistical moralistic Pharisee or a Sadducee who did political business with the powerful; nor a guerrilla who sought the political liberation of his people, nor a contemplative in a monastery. He was a shepherd." Moreover, the pope added, "he spoke his people's language; he was understood, he told the truth, the things of God: he never traded the things of God. But he spoke about them in such a way that the people loved the things of God. That's why they followed him."

Another central point mentioned by the pope was that "Jesus never distances himself from the people and never distances himself from his Father: he was one with the Father." That's how "he had this authority and that's why the people followed him."

"Contemplating Jesus the good shepherd," the pope continued, prompts us to examine our consciences: "Whom do I choose to follow? Those who speak to me about abstract things and with moral casuistry? Those who say they belong to the people of God but are without faith and negotiate everything with the political and economic powers? Those who always want to do odd things, destructive things, engage in so-called wars of liberation, but which in the end are not the Lord's way? Or a remote contemplative?"

That's the key question to ask ourselves: "Whom do I choose to follow? Who convinces me?" A question, Francis concluded, that should lead us to ask "God the Father to bring us close to Jesus, to follow Jesus, to be astounded by what Jesus says."

God's Lullaby

Friday, June 27, 2014
Deuteronomy 7:6-11; Matthew 11:25-30

We have a God "who is in love with us," who strokes us tenderly and sings us a lullaby just as a father does to his baby. Not only that. He seeks us first, he waits for us, he teaches us to become "little," because "love is more in the giving than receiving" and "more in actions than in words." Pope Francis reminded us of this during the Mass celebrated on the morning of Friday, June 27—the feast of the Sacred Heart of Jesus—in the chapel of St. Martha's Guest House.

The pope's meditation took its cue from the Collect read during the liturgy, in which, he said, "we thanked the Lord for giving us the grace, the joy of celebrating in the heart of his Son the great works of his love."

"Love" was the key word chosen by the bishop of Rome to express the deep meaning of the feast of the Sacred Heart. "Today is the feast day of God's love, the love of Jesus Christ: God's love for us and God's love in us." A feast, he added, that "we celebrate with joy."

In particular, the pope said, the "characteristics of love" are two. The first is that "love is more in the giving than receiving"; the second is that "love is more in actions than in words."

"When we say that it's more in the giving than receiving," explained Pope Francis, "it's because love always shares itself, always shares, and the loved one receives it." And "when we say that it's more in actions than in words," he added, it's because "love always gives life, makes something grow."

The pope described the fundamental characteristics of God's love for human beings. He revisited some of the passages read out in the day's liturgy which "twice speak to us of littleness." Indeed, in the first reading, taken from the book of Deuteronomy

(7:6-11), "Moses explains why this people has been chosen and says: because you are the smallest of all nations." Then in Matthew's gospel (11:25-30), "Jesus praises the Father because he has hidden the things of God from the learned and revealed them to little ones."

So, declared the pope, "to understand God's love you need that littleness of heart." Besides, Jesus tells us clearly, if you don't become like children you will not enter the kingdom of heaven. That's the right way: "Become children, become little," because "only in that littleness, in that self-lowering, can you receive" God's love.

It's not accidental, observed the bishop of Rome, that "when he explains how he loves, the Lord himself tries to speak as if talking to a child." God "reminds the people: 'Remember, I taught you to walk as a father teaches his child.'" It's about "that father-child relationship." But, warned the pope, "if you don't become little," that relationship can't happen.

It's a relationship that leads "the Lord in his love for us" to use "words that are like a lullaby." For in the Bible the Lord says: "Don't be afraid, little grub of Israel, don't be afraid!" And he touches us tenderly telling us: "I am with you, I take you by the hand."

That's "the Lord's loving tenderness, that's what he shares with us. It also empowers our own tenderness." But, said the pope, "if we think of ourselves as strong, we will never experience the beauty of the Lord's tenderness."

The "Lord's words make us understand the mysterious love he has for us." Jesus himself shows us what to do. When he speaks about himself, he says he is "gentle and humble of heart." So "he too, God's Son, humbles himself to receive the Father's love."

Another truth that the feast of the Sacred Heart reminds us of, the pope continued, can be gleaned from the passage in the second reading taken from John's first letter (4:7-16): "God loved us first; he always comes before us, he waits for us." The prophet Isaiah "says he is like the almond blossom that flowers first in spring." So, repeated the pope, "when we arrive, he's already there; when we seek him, he has sought us first. He's always ahead of us, he waits to take us into his heart, his love."

Summing up his meditation, Pope Francis said that the two features he had mentioned "can help us understand this mystery of God's love for us: in order to express itself it needs our little-ness, our humility. It also needs our amazement when we seek him and find he's already there waiting for us." For "it's so beau-tiful to understand and feel God's love in Jesus, in the heart of Jesus."

The pope concluded by inviting those present to pray to the Lord to give every Christian the grace "of understanding, feeling, and entering into that mysterious world, to be astounded and find peace in that love which shares itself, gives us joy, and leads us along the way of life like a child led by the hand."

White-Gloved Martyrdom

Monday, June 30, 2014
Matthew 8:18-22

Today is still a time of martyrs. Christians are persecuted in the Middle East where they are killed or forced, "in an el-egant white-gloved way," to flee. On the day when the church re-members the martyrs of the early centuries, Pope Francis invited us to pray "for our brothers and sisters who live under persecution today." Because, he declared, today "there are no fewer martyrs" than in Nero's time. So it was to martyrdom, its occurrence and characteristics today, that the pope devoted the Mass on Monday morning, June 30, in the chapel of St. Martha's Guest House.

"In the prayer at the beginning of the Mass," said the pope, "we prayed: 'Lord, who fed the first shoots of the church of Rome with the blood of martyrs . . .'" That befits the commemoration of the "first martyrs of this church," he explained. Besides, he added, "their bones are nearby, not only in the cemetery, but there are also so many of them buried underground a few meters from here . . . perhaps some even immediately underneath us . . ."

It's particularly significant, noted the pope, that "the word we use in our prayer to the Lord is 'fed': 'You fed the first shoots.'" So "we are talking about the growth of a plant: that makes us think of the many times when Jesus said the kingdom of heaven is like a seed." And "in his first letter, the apostle Peter tells us that we 'have been born again of imperishable seed.'" That "is the seed of God's word. That's what has been sown: the seed is God's word, says the Lord. It is sown."

Jesus explains to us in a parable that "the kingdom of heaven is like a man who had sown seed in the earth, then goes home, rests, works, watches night and day, and the seed grows, sprouts, without him knowing how."

The central question, declared the pope, is to ask ourselves "what to do to make this seed of God's word grow and become the kingdom of God, grow and become church." The bishop of Rome pointed to "the two sources" for this work: "the Holy Spirit—the power of the Holy Spirit—and the witness of Christians."

First of all, explained the pope, "we know that there is no growth without the Spirit; it is he who makes the church, it's he who makes the church grow, it's he who summons the community of the church." But, he continued, "the witness of Christians is also necessary." And "when witness reaches the sticking point, when historical circumstances require strong witness from us, then we get martyrs: the greatest witness of all!" So that's how "this church becomes watered by the blood of martyrs." For "that's the beauty of martyrdom: it begins with witness day after day, and then ends in blood, like Jesus, the first martyr, the first witness, the faithful witness."

In order to be true, witness "must be unconditional," declared the pope. The gospel in today's liturgy (Matthew 8:18-22) is clear about that. "We heard what the Lord said" to the disciple who set a condition on following him: "Lord, first let me go and bury my father." But "the Lord stops him: no!" For, said the pope, "witness must be unconditional, must be firm, must be decisive, must speak the strong language used by Jesus: yes, yes, no, no!" That's precisely "the language of witness."

Looking at the history of "this church of Rome that grows, fed by the blood of martyrs," the pope invited us to think "of all those martyrs today who give their lives for the faith: the persecuted Christians." For, he declared, "if during that persecution by Nero there were such a lot of martyrs, today there are no fewer martyrs, persecuted Christians." The facts are well known. "Think of the Middle East," he said, "the Christians who have to flee from persecution" and "Christians killed by persecutors." And "Christians driven out in an elegant white-gloved way: that is also persecution!"

In our own day, the pope repeated, "there are more witnesses, more martyrs in the church than during the early centuries." And "in our Mass today when we remember our glorious predecessors here in Rome," he invited us also to think about and pray for "our brothers and sisters who are persecuted, who suffer and who, by their blood, make the seed grow of so many little churches that sprout." Yes, he concluded, "let us pray for them and also for ourselves."

MORNING HOMILIES

POPE FRANCIS

"Since Pope Francis's election, I have read
his beautiful morning homilies, and their
publication is something I've long been anticipating
. . . I hope that his surprising insights will lead you
deeper into Scripture and help you encounter
God in a new way."
—*James Martin, S.J.*

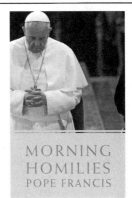

Each morning when Pope Francis celebrates Mass he offers a short homily for fellow residents and guests in the chapel of St. Martha's Guesthouse, where he has chosen to live. Now, the first volume of *Morning Homilies*, which offers reflections from late March through July of 2013, and includes three talks at World Youth Day in Brazil, makes it possible for everyone to experience his lively interpretations of Scripture and his uncanny capacity to engage his listeners, capturing the tenor of daily life.

Francis reflects on the disciples on the road to Emmaus, "simmering their lives in the sauce of their grumbling;" urges Christians to face daily life "ready, like the goalkeeper of a football team, to stop the ball wherever it comes from"; and notes our habit of "going to confession like going to the dry cleaners" as well as the "holy picture face" which we put on to conceal our own sinfulness.

Even more important than these memorable images are the themes that arise again and again in the Pope's preaching: the importance of mercy and forgiveness; the role of Jesus as Savior; the dangers of a church closed in on itself; and the gospel as an unfailing source of life and joy.

224pp., scripture references, softcover.
ISBN 978-1-62698-111-9

ORBIS BOOKS
Maryknoll, New York 10545

From your bookseller or direct: www.orbisbooks.com
Call toll free 1-800-258-5838 M-F 8-4 ET

MORNING HOMILIES II

Pope Francis

"Since Pope Francis's election, I have read
his beautiful morning homilies, and their
publication is something I've long been anticipating
. . . I hope that his surprising insights will lead you
deeper into Scripture and help you encounter
God in a new way."

—*James Martin, S.J.*

Each morning when Pope Francis celebrates Mass he offers a short homily for fellow residents and guests in the chapel of St. Martha's Guesthouse, where he has chosen to live. The second volume of *Morning Homilies*, which offers reflections from August 2013 throught February 2014 makes it possible for everyone to experience his lively interpretations of Scripture and his uncanny capacity to engage his listeners, capturing the tenor of daily life.

Even more important than these memorable images are the themes that arise again and again in the Pope's preaching: the importance of mercy and forgiveness; the role of Jesus as Savior; the dangers of a church closed in on itself; and the gospel as an unfailing source of life and joy.

Also Available
Morning Homilies Volume I
ISBN 978-1-62698-111-9
224pp., scripture references, softcover

ORBIS BOOKS
Maryknoll, New York 10545

From your bookseller or direct: www.orbisbooks.com
Call toll free 1-800-258-5838 M-F 8-4 ET